Fashion Bags & Accesories

LAURENCE KING

First published in Great Britain in 2023 by

Laurence King Student & Professional
An imprint of Quercus Editions Ltd
Carmelite House
50 Victoria Embankment
London EC4Y 0DZ

An Hachette UK company

A CIP catalogue record for this book is available from the British Library

ISBN 978-1-52941-990-0
Ebook ISBN 978-1-52941-991-7

10 9 8 7 6 5 4 3 2 1

Design by Two Sheds
Illustrations by Agnes Virag Moricz

Printed and bound in China by C&C Offset Printing Co., Ltd.

Papers used by Quercus are from well-managed forests and other responsible sources.

Fashion Bags & Accessories

CREATIVE DESIGN & PRODUCTION

Laurence King Publishing

Darla-Jane Gilroy

Introduction — 6

1 Context — 8

The Birth of the Fashion Bag — 10
From Designer Bag to It Bag — 15
The Importance of Fashion Bags — 24
Women's Bags — 25
Men's Bags — 31
Genderless Bags — 36
Luggage — 37

2 Creative Design Process — 40

The Design Cycle — 42
The Brief — 43
CASE STUDY: Stella McCartney — 44
Research — 46
Producing a Concept — 50
Design Development — 52
Design Considerations — 58

3 Drawing — 66

Hand Drawing and Computer Drawing — 68
Drawing for the Design Process — 69
Drawing on the Page — 74
Drawing Bags — 76
The Hand Drawing Toolbox — 83
The Digital Toolbox — 84

4 Materials — 86

Main Materials for Bags — 88
Choosing the Right Materials — 96
Why Leather? — 100
Leather Alternatives — 103

5 Product Development — 114

Transforming a Drawing into a Bag — 116
Sustainable Manufacture — 126

6 Technology and Design — 132

The Digital Fashion Designer — 134
Smart Technology in Fashion
Bags and Accessories — 135
Augmented and Virtual Reality — 139
New Tech Accessories — 141

7 Other Accessories — 146

Flat Accessories — 148
Three-dimensional Accessories — 150
Footwear — 153
Eyewear — 159
Gloves — 162
Belts — 166

8 Professional Development — 168

What Makes a Successful Designer? — 170
Design Education — 171
The Portfolio — 173
Expand Your Horizons — 183
Pathway to Success — 186
INTERVIEW: Alexandra Klimek — 189

Glossary — 194
Index — 196
Credits and acknowledgements — 200

Introduction

Fashion bags, once little more than a functional product, are now true style icons and arguably the most important accessories in the global fashion industry. Fashion bags have become a force that drives innovative design through statement pieces which exist independently of clothing and are a far cry from their origins as practical receptacles.

This book explores fashion bags through approaches to creative design, materials, product development, technological innovation, component design and branding. It also explores the professional development designers need to enter the fashion industry, reviews portfolio development and highlights the business skills that will build a toolbox to get noticed in a competitive industry.

The focus is on classic and new categories of fashion bags, but the book also includes other accessories, such as small leather goods like purses, wallets and cases, as well as footwear, eyewear, gloves and belts.

Chapter 1: Context

Chapter 1 outlines the history of fashion bags and their prominence in the current fashion industry. It covers women's, men's and genderless fashion bags, together with emerging categories of new accessories. It explores the relationship between bags, clothing, footwear and other accessories.

Chapter 2: Creative Design Process

Chapter 2 explores the creative design process, from concept building to trend research as a predictive tool. It considers how visual research can be translated into creative design ideas, and how understanding markets and consumers enables the building of a successful collection of bags.

Chapter 3: Drawing

The focus of Chapter 3 is on drawing to generate ideas, drawing for design development, and technical drawing. It also covers designing, editing and developing a range, and preparing finished presentations. It introduces software packages for design drawing, branding, graphics and portfolio layout.

Chapter 4: Materials

Chapter 4 considers different materials to understand which ones offer the best solutions for different styles of bag. The use of leather as a material for fashion bags and accessories is discussed, as well as the use of sustainable and ethical materials and current alternatives to leather.

Chapter 5: Product Development

Chapter 5 explores how to transform a two-dimensional drawing into a three-dimensional object through standard making techniques, and includes sustainable and ethical ways to develop products.

Chapter 6: Technology and Design

The creative opportunities for bag and accessories design provided by new and emerging technologies are explored in Chapter 6.

Chapter 7: Other Accessories

Chapter 7 considers accessories more broadly by looking at small leather goods, footwear, eyewear, gloves and belts and their status as fashion accessories. It features a useful glossary of terms relating to each type of accessory.

Chapter 8: Professional Development

Chapter 8 considers the attributes a professional designer needs to successfully enter the industry, from education and internships to creating a portfolio, from expanding horizons to next steps and ways into the fashion industry.

1
Context

There is undoubtedly a relationship between the clothes we wear, our shoes and fashion accessories. Changing garment silhouettes and clothing requirements, as well as the development of new materials and manufacturing processes, have all affected how we accessorize outfits.

Bags, shoes, and accessories more generally can have a transformative effect on the wearer because they are worn or carried on the body, so they physically affect the wearer's posture. Such items can also have an aesthetic value that may influence mood. From how they make us feel to what they say about us, fashion accessories have become far more than basic objects for day-to-day living.

Compared to shoes, bags are easily spotted across a crowded room or at a red carpet event. A statement bag shines out like a beacon. Bags also have the added advantage of not being sized, so don't carry many of the negative aspects of sizing that shoes or clothing do. For instance, a bag always fits, regardless of whether a person gains or loses weight, and can also be bought as a gift without having to be tried on for size. In fact, bags have become an ideal partner for any occasion no matter the age, size, gender or lifestyle of the wearer.

The Birth of the Fashion Bag

The first bags were developed for practical reasons because clothes did not have pockets. These bags were small pouches used by both men and women and tied around the waist.

In the seventeenth century, with the rise of thieves and 'cutpurses' (pickpockets who cut purses from waistbands), bags were placed inside men's garments for safe keeping with slits cut into clothing to access them. For practical reasons, these bags became bigger and flatter and eventually were sewn into garments forming a pocket. Most men's bags disappeared, but this was not true of women's garments. Women continued to carry items in small pouches until the beginning of the nineteenth century, when the slender empire line silhouette became fashionable. Women's bags then went from strength to strength, quickly becoming objects denoting status and reflecting the materials and craft techniques of the day in the form of the **reticule**, used to carry fans, visiting cards and money.

By the end of the nineteenth century, the handbag emerged, facilitated by the growth of train travel. Now women needed a small hand-carried bag, which held all their essential belongings. These bags were made of leather because of the material's durability and unique properties which enabled it to withstand cracking and dust, and its ability to be finished in different colours and textures. In fact, leather remains the most popular material for bags with nearly 50 per cent of all bags manufactured globally each year made in leather,

Empire line dress and reticule

10

Art Deco beaded handbag designed by
Maria Likarz-Strauss

although the trend towards more sustainable materials may affect this in the future.

From 1920, a new material, plastic, began to be used to imitate tortoiseshell and ivory, which were commonly used in the frames of bags at the time, and to replicate exotic animal skins as a cheaper alternative to leather.

During the 1920s, bags as fashion accessories slowly evolved, influenced by the changing silhouette of clothing, artistic movements in painting like Cubism, modernist design popularized by the Bauhaus (an influential school of arts and crafts founded in Germany in 1919), and the birth of women's rights. Maria Likarz-Strauss (1893–1971) was a textile designer who worked for the influential Austrian

workshop Wiener Werkstätte throughout the 1920s. Wiener Werkstätte bridged the gap between manufactured products and craft-based traditions. Likarz-Strauss designed bags made of leather and textiles, frequently using nineteenth-century craft beadwork to create her distinctive Art Deco inspired abstract designs. She cleverly used tiny, mass-produced glass beads, updating the technique for the new industrial age.

In America, Charles Whiting (1864–1940) revived the ancient technique of chainmail woven into fine metal handbags. He formed the Whiting & Davis Company in 1896 and throughout the 1900s made mesh bags in sterling silver, gold or vermeil (a gold-plating process over a silver base). Local women knitted the metal links together but in 1912

the process of linking mesh was automated, meaning it could be mass-produced in less expensive metals. This made the company's bags more affordable and throughout the 1920s Whiting & Davis produced metal-linked bags screen-printed with Art Deco designs. They also collaborated with fashion designer Paul Poiret (1879–1944) to make special pieces to go with his collections.

By the late 1920s, plastic had become more prominent and valued in its own right. It was perceived as a contemporary material that captured the spirit of the age because of its versatile properties.

In 1929, Coco Chanel (1883–1971) designed her first hand-carried bag, and during the 1930s rival fashion designer Elsa Schiaparelli (1890–1973) helped cement the relationship between clothing and accessories by creating striking ranges of bags, hats and shoes to go with her surrealist inspired clothes. The pochette, an envelope-style bag carried under the arm, close to the body, later became known as the clutch bag. It is instantly associated with the 1930s, complementing the body conscious bias-cut clothing of the decade. The growing social independence of women reflected their need to carry more things around with them, such as cosmetics, cigarettes and money. Clutch bags were often monogrammed to show the owner's initials. These **monograms** later became the initials of designers and the first form of fashion branding. By 1933 magnetic clasps and zips (zippers) were used to close bags, and by 1934 finger loops were attached to clutch bags, making them easier to carry. From 1937, longer, more practical handles became fashionable and clutches became larger, reflecting the fashion for clothes with wider sleeves.

With the outbreak of World War II in Europe in 1939, handbags entered a more functional yet still fashionable phase. With leather, metal and glass requisitioned for the war effort, the 'make do and mend' years of the war saw fashion bags made from

innovative and repurposed materials and everyday objects. Homemade handbags using craft techniques such as crochet, embroidery and knitting became common, and materials were embellished to imitate patent leather, animal skins and suede. Plastics were cut into strips and woven into intricate designs, and evening bags were made from satin and velvet material decorated with sequins because of the scarcity of glass beads. **Synthetic materials**, lighter than leather, influenced the shapes of handbags, introducing rigid square outlines.

As the 1940s was a time when women started to carry more things around, such as scarves, gloves, cosmetics and perfume, handbags needed to be larger and more functional and, for the first time, bags were carried on the shoulder. On the outbreak of war, department stores started selling gas mask handbags to encourage women to keep their gas masks with them in the event of an attack.

Opposite: Whiting & Davis printed chainmail handbag

Leather 1940s gas mask bag

The no-nonsense handbags of the 1940s war years gave way to the extravagant handbags of the 1947 New Look pioneered by Christian Dior (1905–1957). The post-war economic boom in Europe ignited a revolution in fashion which popularized Dior's co-ordinated, polished look. The New Look reinvented the female silhouette through sculptured jackets and long, full skirts, which still inspire a range of Dior accessories today.

At the beginning of the 1950s, bags returned to their pre-war sizes, becoming more decorative and hand-carried. To boost post-war sales of handbags and other accessories, the trend to match shoes, handbags and clothes was introduced and encouraged by the growth of department stores. Department stores merchandised shoes and handbags together, usually on the ground floor, which ensured customers frequently bought them at the same time as they entered the store. This co-ordinated approach to women's outfits meant a woman required dozens of accessories to match the clothes in her wardrobe.

Throughout the 1950s new materials were developed, such as Lucite, a transparent acrylic material used to create evening bags. Bamboo was also made fashionable by Gucci, who used it to make handles for its bags.

Lady with bamboo handled bag, 1957

From Designer Bag to It Bag

The first designer bags were developed to supplement designer clothes, through classic bags such as the Kelly from Hermès. This bag was named after Grace Kelly (1929–1982), the film star and style icon of the day, who always carried it.

Prince Rainier of Monaco and his wife Grace Kelly with the Hermès Kelly bag, named in her honour

In 1955, Coco Chanel revolutionized designer handbags with an updated version of her 1929 bag, renamed the 2.55 bag (named after the month, February, and year 1955, when it was first launched). This turned wearing bags on the shoulder into a fashion statement and not just a necessity, and introduced the idea of carrying a bag hands-free to women who had previously carried handbags by stiff top handles. This changed the way fashion bags were carried forever and heralded the dawn of the decorative shoulder bag, which was taken up by Gucci in the 1960s with the Jackie O Bouvier bag.

Reflecting a marked period of social change, the 1960s were characterized by a more practical and functional approach to fashion, which promoted more informal ways of wearing clothes. This resulted in a focus on pockets, making fashion bags less of a necessity and more of a luxury item.

Chainmail shoulder bag by Paco Rabanne

Film star Audrey Hepburn with the Louis Vuitton Speedy 25 bag

Film star Audrey Hepburn (1929–1993), who had traditionally been dressed by French fashion house Givenchy, turned to Louis Vuitton for her handbags. As a busy Hollywood star, Hepburn frequently travelled by air, and she collaborated with Vuitton to create a smaller version of the Speedy bag. The Speedy 25 could be flattened easily and packed in a suitcase, making it the ideal bag to carry while travelling. The Speedy 25 perfectly reflected Hepburn's fast-paced jet set lifestyle and remains one of Vuitton's best-selling bags today.

In 1969, Paco Rabanne (b. 1934) presented a range of stunning metal shoulder bags and belts alongside his clothing collection. Rabanne used his knowledge of jewellery to spearhead the use of metal and plastic for both clothing and accessories. This collection firmly established the fashion bag as a statement piece within a collection.

The concept of statement bags was picked up by Mary Quant (b. 1930) and Bárbara Hulanicki (b. 1936), founder of Biba, an influential London fashion store of the 1960s and 1970s. Both designers offered more affordable versions of fashion bags for the high street that reflected the style of 1960s models, actresses and musicians, such as Twiggy (b. 1949), Edie Sedgwick (1943–1971), Françoise Hardy (b. 1944) and Cher (b. 1946).

Opposite: Jackie Onassis carrying the Gucci Jackie O Bouvier bag

1960s model Twiggy wears chainmail belt and leather shoulder bags

Hippie culture of the 1970s had a marked effect on bags, which became less structured and worn on long straps across the body. Softer leather and suede became popular, along with fabrics such as silk and velvet, embellished with prints and embroidery. Techniques like patchwork, and trimmings such as tassels and fringing, became signatures of bags in the early 1970s. Designer brands, like Ralph Lauren, still reference 1970s hippie chic in their collections today.

Emilio Pucci (1914–1992) applied his unmistakable bright psychedelic prints onto silk and velvet fabrics, which he used to make clutches and shoulder bags. In 1975, Loewe launched the Amazona, an unlined bag that became synonymous with a nomadic, hedonistic lifestyle.

Emilio Pucci printed silk bag with a metal shoulder strap

By 1977, disco culture took hold in music and fashion, reflecting a more self-indulgent and glamorous style of dress – the antithesis of hippie culture. American designer Halston (1932–1990) was at the centre of the New York disco scene. He popularized jersey fabrics in his free-flowing clothing designs, which were perfect to dance in and were accompanied by a small metal mesh bag by the Whiting & Davis Company to hold the essentials for a night out. The Whiting & Davis bag became the must-have item of the late 1970s and early 1980s. This was not the first time that Whiting & Davis bags had become style icons; the company's trademark chainmail bags go back to 1896 and their Art Deco inspired designs and collaborations with fashion designers made them famous throughout the 1920s and 1930s (see page 13).

Over the subsequent decades of the 1980s and 1990s, designer handbags gradually evolved from iconic pieces, which remained constant for decades, to the trend-driven designs we see today.

The 1980s engendered a period of excess, reflected in a maximalist design styling. During the period, handbags became a key means of communicating style and status through ostentatious design and branding. Dior's top-handled tote bag had an oversized Dior logo charm added to it and was renamed the Lady Dior in honour of Princess Diana (1961–1997), the most influential style icon of the time. Chanel replaced the traditional Mademoiselle twist-lock on their flip quilted-top bag in favour of the interlocking CC logo, originally designed by Coco Chanel herself. Fendi's logo, created by Karl Lagerfeld (1933–2019) in 1965 when he first worked for the house, was relaunched onto painted canvas, previously only used to line travel trunks. This **signature print** (a print original to a brand) was used on the body of bags, along with an unmissable FF metal clasp fastening, creating a more contemporary and playful image for the brand.

Leather Birkin bag by Hermès

In 1984, Hermès created the Birkin, named in honour of the film star Jane Birkin (b. 1946), which has become one of the most recognized and expensive bags in the world. The tight control of the production and sales of the Birkin has fuelled an enormous second market for sales of the bag, prompting commentators to suggest that an investment in a designer Birkin bag may be a better investment than in gold. The Birkin went on to set the record for the most expensive bag ever sold.

Since 1919, Prada has been the official supplier to the Italian royal family, displaying the House of Savoy coat of arms and knotted rope design on their logo. In 1983, Miuccia Prada (b. 1949) set a new standard for luxury handbags by using nylon fabric, normally used by the Italian army, to create a new brand image for Prada which combined traditional and contemporary elements.

The trademark triangular Prada metal logo was added onto a utilitarian inspired range of designer bags made from signature nylon fabric that redefined what a luxury fashion bag could be. Prada's black nylon rucksack, worn by both men and women, became the ultimate status symbol in the 1980s and early 1990s and the first genderless bag.

Carrie Bradshaw (Sarah Jessica Parker) with the Fendi Baguette

The 1990s marked an era where fashion bags were mythologized through popular culture, including music and TV shows of the time. The Fendi Baguette, launched in 1997, was carried under the arm like a long loaf or baguette of French bread, creating a silhouette not seen since the 1930s. This reflected a casual approach to carrying designer bags that rejected the historically ladylike connotations of a handbag.

If Prada bags were about function, the Baguette was aspirational and exclusive. Carrie Bradshaw, the fictional character in the TV series *Sex and the City*, popularized the Baguette (the bag was famously stolen from her in one episode) and made it the first bag to have a significant waiting list. The bag's simple shape and conspicuous FF clasp made it both recognizable and possible to reinvent. The bag has been produced in over 600 fabrics and colours thanks to its regular appearances on *Sex and the City*. The Fendi Baguette became the first must-have IT bag.

All designer labels want to launch an IT bag each season that becomes an indispensable part of every woman's wardrobe. Through the 2000s the fashion bag has become an ever-changing, covetable item typified through fashion brands. Prada's 1950s inspired Bowling Bag appeared in 2000 and, such was its success, it was reissued in 2012. It continued Prada's tradition of elevating the everyday into something exceptional. The petite-sized Fendi Baguette remained popular throughout the 2000s and was widely copied. Louis Vuitton's collaborations with Stephen Sprouse (1953–2004) contrasted street culture and couture to create bold, graffiti-like luggage and bags in 2001.

Stephen Sprouse graffiti luggage for Louis Vuitton, inspired by street culture

Rihanna with Alexander Wang Rocco bag

Louis Vuitton went on to collaborate with artist Takashi Murakami (b. 1962). Murakami's signature repeated motifs, such as his cherry blossom flower emblem, represent his Japanese heritage. His designs have been intertwined with the Louis Vuitton signature motif in the Cherry Blossom collection, adorning a selection of Vuitton's classic bag styles.

The Dior equestrian inspired, top-handled saddle bag, also adopted by Carrie Bradshaw's character in *Sex and the City*, was an instant success. The pouch-style saddle bag appears in endless permutations of colour and fabric and has been adapted for the Dior men's range. Chloé's slouchy oblong-shaped Paddington bag was defined by an enormous padlock fastening. The bag weighed a hefty 1 kg (2¼ lbs) when empty, but still inspired numerous imitations and pre-sold 8,000 units, making it one of the most sought-after IT bags of its day. Another weighty bag was Alexander Wang's Rocco. Edgy and versatile, it tipped the scales at 1.4 kg (3 lbs) due to its heavy, stud-embellished base.

Balenciaga introduced the Motorcycle bag in the early 2000s as a prototype for a catwalk show. The lightweight bag, reminiscent of a worn biker jacket, combined soft leather, studs, buckles and zips pulled by long leather tassels. Its lack of a logo was a departure from many other bags of the time. The bag relied instead on edgy metal **hardware**, such as studs and rings, and on high-quality leather to drive its desirability.

Balenciaga Motorcycle bag

Dior's Saddle bag

Paddington bag by Chloé

The Importance of Fashion Bags

'My guilty pleasure is bags. I don't even have a clue how many I own.'

Poppy Delevingne, model and actress

Since the start of the twenty-first century, fashion bags and accessories have been the main source of income for many luxury houses and designer brands. The global luxury fashion bag market size was valued at $58.3 billion in 2018 and is expected to reach $89.9 billion by 2026.

Fashion bags are not only lucrative but also an important way of increasing brand recognition, as they show the personality of a brand. Branding ranges from the discreet elegance of Hermès to the more ostentatious branding of Louis Vuitton's monogrammed pieces, although both signify the affluence of the bags' owners. Branding adds appeal and builds meaningful communication with consumers to further a brand's image and positioning. This is why subtle or unsubtle branding is essential to all fashion bags.

The best brand logos have longevity and work in a variety of different mediums. They can appear in different forms on one product – stamped into a buckle, embossed in leather, woven into the lining, or printed onto the outer body of a bag. Logos must translate across different cultures, geography and languages. They can also be aligned with a colour or interchanged with a print, symbol or slogan. Chanel's interlocked C, Nike's swoosh, Burberry's check, Tiffany's patent-protected blue, and Coach's horse and carriage logo are all highly globally recognizable.

Quilted leather Chanel shoulder bag with interlocking double C logo

Women's Bags

'A Fendi bag and a bad attitude – That's all I need to get me in a good mood.'

Around The Way Girl, LL Cool J

A bag can be a powerful addition to an outfit, making it more stylish and original or more practical and functional. The right bag changes the emphasis of an outfit by adding character, and can be a timeless icon because of its style or make a bold statement through its colour or material. An integral part of a woman's daily routine, a bag can provide a means of self-expression that is less self-conscious than clothing. Many women, for example, are happy to choose a brightly coloured accessory but take a more cautious approach to the colour of their garments.

A designer bag can be a wise investment; while clothing loses its value quickly, a bag can hold or even increase its value. The unit price of a designer bag now easily exceeds that of clothing. It can make a perfect first impression because the bag chosen tells others how the wearer wants to be perceived, not only through the brand, but also through the style of bag, which can be delicately hand-held or slung casually over a shoulder.

All bags make a unique outward statement about a woman's social independence because they reflect her move away from the domestic setting. Urban environments, such as offices, bars, restaurants, theatres, red carpet events, sports or travel (whether a long weekend away or a round the world trip), all need bags with different functions but also bags that make a statement about a woman's personality, values, lifestyle, independence, social status, knowledge of fashion or earning power. A functional backpack, for example, says something different to an evening clutch bag.

Women's accessories continue to gain prominence in the current fashion landscape for different reasons, but one key factor is the increasing number of women who work, driving the growth of contemporary 'sac de jour', or day bags. As well as traditional **small leather goods**, defined as items such as purses, wallets and sunglasses cases, women carry many more work-related items like laptops, phones, tablets and chargers, as well as personal possessions, with them every day and have a range of bag styles to choose from. These bags not only perform on a functional level but also say something about the character of the wearer.

Bags have been closely aligned with celebrities and their aspirational lifestyles since the 1920s. The endorsements of celebrities, and those of influencers and bloggers posting on social media about the newest items, have also fuelled interest in fashion bags, guiding consumers through a new kind of purchasing journey. Brands are taking advantage of this growing power of celebrity endorsement and influencers to continually update consumers on new products.

Many women have a favourite style of handbag which they carry on a regular basis, one that is versatile and connects with a particular attitude or lifestyle. But what are the key contemporary bag styles and what do they say about those who use them?

ReKnit tote bag by Everlane

Leather handbag with side pocket and carry handles

Tote Bag

The humble tote bag appears in every bag range and accounts for nearly 42 per cent of global handbag sales each year. Because of its generous proportions and internal space, which allows room to carry relevant items, the tote bag is the most popular handbag used on a daily basis by working women. Totes are rectangular portrait or landscape shaped bags with long double handles and a well-organized interior designed to contain everything from a favourite lipstick to a laptop. They can be a lightweight, foldaway nylon bag or a much more desirable leather construction complete with branded handbag charms.

Signature tote bags
Le Pliage by Longchamp
Saffiano by Michael Kors
Everyday XS by Balenciaga
Muse by Saint Laurent

Hand-held Handbag

A bag that gets noticed, a hand-held handbag is a medium-sized day bag that is bigger than a clutch or baguette bag and is designed to hold everyday essentials and personal items. Hand-held handbags have either one single top handle or a pair of handles, giving them a demure and less functional feel than other bags. They come in a range of styles, such as the trapeze, accordion or inset gusset, and can also have metal frames to fasten them.

Signature hand-held handbags
Nano by Celine
City by Balenciaga
The Kelly by Hermès
Lady Dior by Dior
The Stam by Marc Jacobs

Gabbi shoulder bag by JW Pei

Leather clutch bag with Karl Lagerfeld metal logo detail

Shoulder Bag

A shoulder bag is one of the most popular shapes at the luxury end of the market. It can be carried on the shoulder but does not have long enough straps to be carried across the body. It is adaptable and can translate from a busy day at the office to drinks at night, being both a comfortable and a coverable bag that is often a smaller diversification of a hand-held handbag.

Signature shoulder bags
K/Signature by Karl Lagerfeld
Braided handle shoulder bag by Prada
TB Mini by Burberry
Hunting 9 by The Row
Loulou Toy by Saint Laurent

Clutch

A clutch is a small hand-held bag without straps or handles, but occasionally it may have a carrying loop attached that can slip neatly round the wrist. Slimmer than other styles, a clutch is less practical and only fits the essentials. Clutches are more usually associated with evening or special occasion bags because of their size. By virtue of the way they are carried they can be sedate, reflecting a ladylike elegance, or show a total disregard for convention if held casually.

Signature clutch bags
Rockstud Envelope by Valentino
Slim Slide by Judith Leiber
Pouch Intrecciato by Bottega Veneta
Régine by Bienen-Davis, metallic brocade minaudière

Leather Fendi Baguette bag

Embossed leather Hobo bag with adjustable shoulder strap

Baguette Bag

The baguette is a narrow, compact bag, like an oversized clutch bag, which either zips shut or has a flap closure. Its short strap enables it to be carried under the arm, close to the body. Originally launched by Fendi in 1997 to be a style of bag that can be endlessly reinvented, it appealed instantly to the hedonists of the late 1990s. Initially the bag was considered too small to be commercially viable, but the baguette has become so successful that it is now a bag style in its own right and maintains its reputation for decadent glamour.

Signature baguette bags
Baguette by Fendi
Multicoloured nylon by Prada
Cherry print by Louis Vuitton
Rachel Bag by Far

Hobo

The Hobo, as its name suggests, has a casual aesthetic designed to reflect a free-spirited, easy-going, spontaneous lifestyle. The construction of the body of the bag is informal and slouchy so it suits soft, supple materials, which give the Hobo a casual appearance. It has a carry strap so it can rest easily on the shoulder and is perfect for travel.

Signature Hobo bags
Jackie O by Gucci
Hadley by Coach
BV Jodie by Bottega Veneta

Leather crossbody bag with patterned flap

Weekender with double zip details and contrast straps

Crossbody Bag

The crossbody bag is perfect for day-to-day use for a secure 'hands-free' style that sits comfortably across the body, with a flap to make accessing contents easy but also keeping items secure. This is a versatile bag made in several sizes, from the smaller saddle or canteen-style bags which hold essentials such as a phone, wallet, keys and make-up, to the medium-sized more versatile messenger-style bag.

Signature crossbody bags
Rainbow Circle by Coach
Gate by Loewe
Camera by Balenciaga
GV3 by Givenchy
TB by Burberry

Weekender

A weekender is a larger version of a tote bag with a wider base and usually made of leather or a lightweight material. The bags come in a range of styles, such as the barrel-shaped duffel bag, the sports inspired bowling bag or the rectangular style of the classic weekender. Weekenders are stylish and convenient and, in response to the growth in short weekend breaks, have replaced more conventional hard luggage and suitcases.

Signature weekenders
Bowling bag by Prada
GG embossed holdall by Gucci
Speedy 35 by Louis Vuitton

Qwstion backpack in Banatex

Leather Cambridge Satchel Co. X Comme des Garçons satchel with double buckle fastening and shoulder strap

Backpack

Backpacks, also called rucksacks or knapsacks, are functional bags dating back to 1910. They have two straps enabling them to be carried on the back or slung over one shoulder, with small pouch pockets on the outside body so essentials can be reached easily. Backpacks have earned a reputation as a practical bag for sporty, outdoor activities but are now made to fit a wide variety of needs, whether for commuting, going to the gym or travelling.

Made in leather, canvas and nylon, the backpack was reinvented as a luxury bag by Prada in the 1980s and is a staple of most fashion bag ranges, sitting happily in urban surroundings.

Signature backpack
Prada

Satchel

The classic leather satchel is still reminiscent of the functional brown leather bags used to carry books by school children for more than a hundred years. This unlined leather bag has a back section that extends to create a flap fastening across a front pocket with a metal buckle. Occasionally the satchel construction can also have a double strap in the middle of the bag so it can be carried like a backpack. This unassuming bag was given a fashion makeover by the Cambridge Satchel Co. in 2008. The company produces handmade timeless designs in a vibrant colour range, and went on to collaborate with Comme des Garçons.

Signature satchel
The Cambridge Satchel Co. X Comme des Garçons

Men's Bags

Since the end of the twentieth century, men have been liberated from the confines of the suit, a uniform they had been bound to for over a hundred years. Through the casualization of their clothing and a dress-down culture at work, men have begun to experiment with their appearances and inevitably become more interested in accessories.

Men's accessories come from a tradition of expensive items usually personalized through monogramming, such as pocket squares and cufflinks, or functional briefcases and luggage. While these particular luxury items may not have been accessible to everyone, and that remains true to some extent, it is a misconception that bags are largely the domain of women. Through the rise of portable technology, men, just like women, are carrying much more around with them than they used to. Bags offer them an exciting extra layer of self-expression, as well as solving the practical problems of transporting items.

The large growth in the market for men's fashion bags has been led by the firm favourite, the messenger bag, which accommodates a laptop and a plethora of smaller items like wallets, key fobs and glasses cases.

Watch straps and desk accessories that bridge fashion and interior design pieces have also become more prominent as new categories of accessories are emerging to keep pace with technology (see page 144). These revolve around small tech cases, and although these pocket-sized items do not have the impact of a statement bag, they are more affordable than larger pieces,

providing an entry point into a brand and, thus, a branding opportunity for fashion labels.

Men's fashion bags include many of the same styles as women's, for example the tote, messenger and backpack, but the weekender takes on a decidedly sportier persona and often appears in men's ranges as a chunky holdall including specially designed pockets for football (soccer) boots and gym kit, as well as being perfect for short travel breaks. Document cases and briefcases, both traditional men's accessories, have been re-imagined into contemporary items using less-rigid materials like lightweight nylon and canvas. The most noticeable differences compared to women's fashion bags across all styles are the scaling up of bags into larger, more generous proportions, resizing of hardware including metal buckles, fastenings and zips, and an emphasis on functional lightweight materials like waxed cotton, nylon and canvas. Details, such as reinforced stitching at stress points on a bag, also highlight a more functional approach to design for men's fashion bags because men tend to buy fewer bags and use them for longer.

Men have moved away from standard black or brown to more colourful palettes used by designers

31

Model wears Dior signature Saddle bag

like Paul Smith, Mulberry and Burberry. Tan, grey, navy, green and burgundy have become the new staples for men's bags, along with accent colours like red, orange and citrus yellow. Some men's fashion bags have been adapted from women's ranges and masculinized with details such as crossbody straps, for example the Dior signature Saddle bag and the Loewe Puzzle bag. Others have been 'acquired', like the Hermès Birkin, to blur the lines between genders.

Men, like women, favour styles of bags for day-to-day use that reflect both practicality and personality.

WANT Les Essentiels tote bag

Mulberry nylon zipped weekender with leather straps

Tote Bag

The multifunctional tote bag is popular with men and women. The upscaled men's version is made in leather, nylon or workwear inspired denim, as a less formal alternative to a briefcase-style bag. It offers ease of access to the interior of the bag with well-organized internal pockets and compartments and sometimes has a detachable shoulder strap.

Signature men's tote bags
Gucci
WANT Les Essentiels
Paul Smith
Print denim tote bag by Dsquared2

Weekender

A weekender is a roomy holdall-style men's bag with the attributes of a suitcase and backpack in one bag. It is perfect for business trips and short weekend breaks. It has carry handles so it can be hand-held or worn on the shoulder and sometimes has a detachable shoulder strap. A double-ended zip for easy access, button-down sides that can be released to make more room when needed, and a soft construction that allows it to fold flat are practical features which make the bag functional and contemporary.

Signature weekenders
Zipped weekender by Mulberry
Canvas keepall Bandoulière by Louis Vuitton
Weekender by Troubadour
Grand Ambition weekender by Cole Haan

Barbour messenger bag

Nylon backpack with zip detail and carry handle

Messenger Bags

The messenger bag is perfect for active lifestyles. Worn across the body to leave hands free, the bag is ideal for busy professionals. Often the style is adapted to a particular function, like the camera messenger or the city messenger. Bigger than its female counterpart, a men's messenger bag easily accommodates a laptop and is more durable, with protective padding inside, interior divider pockets, a secure flap and zip fastening. A strongly utilitarian bag, it has its design origins in the DeMartini Global Canvas Company of the 1950s.

Signature messenger bags
Puzzle by Loewe
Nova Check by Burberry
Mailbag leather messenger by Barbour

Backpack

The backpack was given a luxury facelift by designer brand Prada, selling to both men and women and becoming a staple in fashion bag ranges. The bag can be carried hands-free on the back for even weight distribution or over one shoulder, making it ideal for urban and rural settings. Its adjustable padded double straps and practical external pockets make it functional and stylish.

Signature backpacks
Master Piece by Prada
Eastpak
Herschel Supply Co.
Sandqvist

Leather document case with soft double handles

Leather briefcase with brass flap fastening and top carry handle

Document Holder

A document holder is a hand-held contemporary alternative to a briefcase which is smart enough to look businesslike without being overly formal. It will fit a tablet or small laptop alongside important documents organized through internal dividers. Features include a zip for security and protective padding for tech and electronic devices. Document holders are more popular in men's ranges of accessories but do sometimes appear in women's ranges too.

Signature document holders
Smythson
Tom Ford
Common Projects
Comme des Garçons

Briefcase

The traditional attaché-style briefcase has a dated image linked to grey-suited accountants and bankers. In its solid, boxy guise it has fallen out of favour because of its excessive weight and cumbersome interior that does not accommodate today's portable technology. The contemporary briefcase has been reborn using softer leather and a streamlined silhouette, but still retains an air of formality, sturdy carry handles and a zip or lock fastening.

Signature briefcases
Dunhill
Smythson
Bottega Veneta

Genderless Bags

'Inclusivity is the new norm and fashion has to be a part of that.'

Bradley Miller, influencer and activist

The growing power of social media has spotlighted a more fluid approach to masculinity and femininity. Brands, both niche and mainstream, have begun to regard gender neutral or non-gendered products as the norm and not the exception. The fashion industry is exploring gender using a new narrative that goes beyond terms like 'androgynous' and 'unisex'.

In an attempt to reframe our understanding of gender in relation to clothes, accessories and footwear, influential brands such as Gucci, Louis Vuitton, Maison Margiela and Thom Browne, and more moderately priced H&M, have been prominent in the discussion around gender, taking positive steps towards less gender-specific dressing. These brands are positioning themselves as relevant to a generation of people who no longer see gender as a defining factor. This reflects a move within the industry to be more representative of consumers who expect brands to meet their expectations of inclusion and social justice.

On the catwalk there has been a broader and more representative choice of model, breaking away from preconceived views of masculinity and femininity. Genderless fragrances and cosmetics have also been launched and non-binary categories have been added to global fashion trade shows as the number of designers whose collections do not delineate by gender continues to grow.

While it is unlikely the future of bags will be truly genderless, some designers are spearheading a different approach to non-gendered products.

They may follow conventional design approaches to create products, but they also conceive them as fashion bags anyone can buy and use. The idea of the boyfriend bag, jeans or jacket, where items of traditionally male clothing are worn by women, is well-established. More recently though, in what has come to be known as the 'Birkin Boy' phenomena, it is no longer unusual to see a man carrying a handbag by Hermès, Dior, Fendi or Chanel that was traditionally considered to be for a woman.

Reece Morgan with bags by Hermès and Chanel

Luggage

Traditional hard luggage and briefcases have largely gone out of fashion due to their design and weight, and the advent of less glamorous ways to travel. Most contemporary brands, however, offer a combination of structured and soft luggage and cases for both men and women. Soft luggage has the advantage of more storage space and the flexibility to expand internal storage pockets to pack a wider range of items, but offers less protection than sturdier hard luggage. Generally soft luggage is lighter, but the introduction of durable materials, for example polycarbonate (a combination of plastic and carbon), provide a hard structure without adding weight. The most popular luggage styles are cases on wheels that can be easily pulled along.

Signature luggage
Carry case by Away
Samsonite
Kipling
Yeti

Hard sided carry on with glide wheels

The deep-rooted conventions of bland, outdated unisex bags are being supplanted by modern interpretations of gender-neutral ranges by brands like Telfar, which has come to prominence through its embossed shoulder bag bearing the slogan 'Not For You, For Everyone', and Thom Browne, whose micro pouch in sporty black nylon, worn around the neck, not only satisfies the trend toward micro accessories but also gender neutrality.

Designer Telfar Clemens (b. 1985) describes his brand as 'Horizontal, democratic and universal'. His gender-neutral basics bags are made from 100 per cent vegan leather, embossed with the Telfar TC logo, and come in three sizes with carry handles and a shoulder strap, making them perfect for formal and functional uses. In an era of social media, Telfar has become synonymous with wider representation in the fashion industry, where the brand has been described as 'genderless, democratic, and transformative'.

Some products, like Globe-Trotter luxury travel cases, have always held a genderless status, appealing to both men and women by virtue of their function. Globe-Trotter has remained relevant through the integrity of its craft heritage and traditional manufacture techniques. The brand's stylish yet simple aesthetic make the cases modern classics that improve with age. Thanks to a string of successful collaborations, most notably with Paul Smith and Tiffany & Co., the cases continue to appeal to younger, more eclectic audiences.

Marc Jacobs with a Chanel quilted bag

Telfar shopper

Globe-Trotter X Paul Smith

Globe-Trotter sky-blue cases

2
Creative Design Process

Creative design is a personal journey to seek inspiration and create new thinking. It requires discipline, curiosity, determination and the skills to interpret information in unusual and original ways. Although there are many different market levels at which products are created and sold within the fashion industry, and a huge range of different types of products being designed and manufactured, the design process is largely the same and follows a logical sequence of tasks that have clear start and finish points. Each task interlinks to create a continuous design cycle.

In a large company a designer sticks to clear lines of responsibility in relation to the design process, which may be split over several departments. In a smaller business or design studio with fewer people, a single designer may be involved in more aspects of the design process. Creative design is, however, a collaborative practice where designers create products as part of a team or collaborate with specialists, sometimes having to compromise to reach common agreement and create the best products.

The Design Cycle

The design cycle starts with research, inquiry and analysis to produce a concept that can be used to generate design ideas in response to the brief. These ideas are then refined and lead to the development of products that answer the brief and are grouped together to create collections of items with similar characteristics. Finally, these collections are evaluated and the findings inform the next cycle of design.

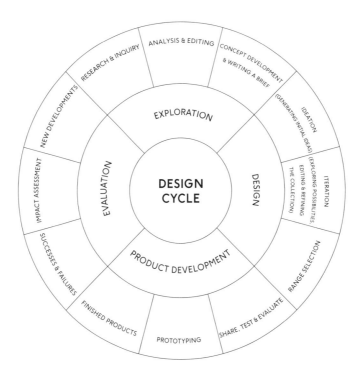

Through the **design cycle** individual designers start to develop a personal style and design handwriting that becomes immediately recognizable. With practice and experience the design process becomes quicker and easier and the design handwriting of each new collection becomes more established.

Each new collection must be ingrained in a concept, the starting point for which could be a vintage piece, an old photograph, a book or film. No matter what the source of inspiration, it must provide a solid grounding from which to investigate and collect ideas.

The Brief

The design process starts with a brief, a document that sets the parameters for a design project. Provided by a client or self-generated by a designer, a brief lays out specific requirements related to the outcomes a designer must meet. For example, a brief would typically include the number and type of products in a range, the techniques and materials to be used, the target audience or consumer, and the budget and timeline.

Briefs should be approached with a flexible, open mind. Following experimental processes is key to discovering new ways of designing and creating products. This experimentation can sometimes revolve around the revival of traditional craft skills or the application of new emerging technologies, or even a combination of both.

Once a brief is set, designers are expected to undertake research and produce a creative response that is not only about understanding the aesthetic appeal of a particular brand or its function, but also the wider cultural landscape within which it fits, including its relationship to competitor brands. An overview and understanding of all levels of the market – luxury, designer, high street, or niche brands – helps to connect with specific consumers to establish their requirements at each market level. Understanding the demands of a particular audience or group of consumers makes sure a product is relevant to them and successfully conveys the values of the brand.

Designers need to understand the technicalities and cost of manufacturing that determine how a product is made, the materials used, design detailing, and techniques or traditional craft skills used, in order to consider how these can be adapted for a

contemporary consumer. They also need to be aware of project milestones to meet deadlines set within a brief, and allow time to reflect on and fine-tune a product. Making sure essential tasks are completed at the right time ensures the demands of the **supply chain** (the sequence of processes involved in the production and distribution of a product) are met and a product can be man-ufactured and sold each season.

Increasing sustainability is at the forefront of design thinking. It is essential to understand and reflect on a **product's life cycle** (the stages a product goes through from its development to its decline and disappearance), and current issues such as **slow fashion** and **ethical production**. Slow fashion is a way to stem overproduction and overconsumption by producing fewer, better-quality items that consider the resources required and the process of manufacture. Ethical production and social justice spotlight a range of issues about how products are made and under what conditions, with the aim of making production less exploitative and more sustainable (see pages 50, 58–9, 126–31).

CASE STUDY: Stella McCartney

About the Brand

Stella McCartney was born in London in 1971 to rock legend Paul McCartney and photographer and animal rights campaigner, Linda McCartney. She studied fashion design at Central Saint Martins and graduated in 1995, quickly establishing herself within the industry. By 1997 she had been appointed as the Creative Director of Chloé in Paris and is credited for the critical and commercial success of the house.

In 2001, Stella McCartney took the step to launch her own fashion label, beginning a 17-year partnership with the French luxury conglomerate Kering to create what would become the world's first vegan luxury brand.

Brand Values

Throughout her career, Stella McCartney has championed environmental awareness, sustainability, animal rights and social justice. True to her values she never uses leather, feathers, fur, or animal products in any of her collections. She follows the UN Guiding Principles on Business and Human Rights, a global standard regarding corporate business ethics in relation to human rights, which she uses as a framework for best practice in her business.

Her brand continues to grow its commitment to sustainability and social justice through an innovative approach to materials sourcing, manufacture and supply chain considerations, partnerships, and collaborations, always striving to create a more equitable and sustainable fashion system. Her successful collaborations include adidas, H&M and the Ellen MacArthur Foundation.

Stella McCartney has admitted that it is difficult to design without using traditional materials, but she has successfully sourced effective alternatives. Her bags and accessories use a blend of organic and synthetic fibres with vegetable coatings, eco-friendly materials like ECONYL® (made from recycled fishing nets), and recycled plastics. In 2009 she developed a luxury fashion bag, her iconic Falabella (see page 107), creating the first prestigious vegan fashion bag ever produced.

Sustainability

In 2015 the brand announced its First Global Environmental Profit and Loss Account, in which overall environmental impact of materials used was reduced by 35 per cent over a three-year period while enjoying the best business performance of the brand since its launch, proving that it was possible to be sustainable and profitable at the same time.

Her sustainable initiatives have sparked interest within the Kering Group, which owns Gucci, Bottega Veneta and Alexander McQueen, helping sustainability to gain momentum and show how the industry could scale the concept. In 2021 Kering was ranked in the top 10 of the most sustainable companies in the world in The Global 100 environmental index compiled by media and investment company Corporate Knights.

Stella McCartney uses every opportunity to reflect the brand's values, including in her advertising campaigns. In Autumn/Winter 2017 her advertising campaign was shot in collaboration with Swiss fine artist and photographer Urs Fischer (b. 1973) to explore the concept of waste and consumption. Fischer shot her collection using a Scottish landfill site as a backdrop.

The Frayme Mylo™ by Stella McCartney

In 2019, Stella McCartney entered a partnership with LVMH to further develop her brand and serve as a special advisor on sustainability to LVMH's executive committee.

In 2021 LVMH announced plans to build a research centre in Saclay, France. The centre will be dedicated to researching sustainable production, new materials, innovative biotechnologies and digital data leading to a reduced carbon footprint and more eco-friendly practices.

Stella McCartney continues to be vocal about the future of fashion and the fashion industry's animal cruelty and environmental impact. In 2021, 80 per cent of her women's collection was made from sustainable materials, including forest-friendly viscose, KOBA® fur-free fur, sustainable beech and repurposed fabrics. The collection, entitled 'Our time has come', was a lighthearted depiction of animals rewilding London but communicated a serious message of animal rights and equality to end the fur trade globally. The collection also included a maxi version of the Falabella, and the Frayme saddle-style bag with a chunky gold and silver-tone chain forming the handle. In 2022, the Frayme Mylo became the first bag created in mycelium to be sold commercially.

Research

Creative design relies on research both for inspiration to generate original ideas and for knowledge of the technical skills which inform how products are made. Research and technical understanding enable a designer to successfully develop a product from a two-dimensional drawn idea into a three-dimensional product.

Excellent research skills are required to find information, but as information is so readily available through the internet and social media channels, designers must also have the ability to filter information, selecting the most relevant pieces of research and interpreting these into an original concept.

Designers carry out layers of research. Initially research will be conducted to establish a concept. Once this is defined, further research is undertaken to inspire design ideas, to source appropriate materials, hardware, embellishments or other techniques, and to understand the client, market and context in which designs will sit.

The key to successfully designing a collection is the depth and spread of the research undertaken. Research should never be confined to a particular discipline and should always take an expansive approach to explore different historical and cultural responses to accessories, embellishment, function and how accessories are carried. Many designers revisit specific historical moments or have recurrent research themes, which underpin their personal style and design handwriting.

Analysing and editing research is a skill in itself; the process ensures that the most important and stimulating nuggets of information are taken forward. Once research has been gathered it can be edited by creating research themes – inspirational, consumer, market, technical and contextual.

It is important to factor in the amount of time it may take to create and develop each research theme. If a particular material or process is not available in the right colour or at the right price point, or cannot be produced at the right time, this may have an impact on the design and manufacture of a collection. Research may need to be re-examined in order to make amendments to a concept and to the collection.

It is essential that a designer develops the ability to analyse and edit information to create new solutions that are innovative. This requires several things: a designer needs to understand the requirements of an individual brief or brand and also have a huge amount of wider knowledge. Being able to understand cultural, social, economic and ethical considerations, as well as new emerging technologies which may influence design, drives innovation. A designer also needs to be aware of established and niche brands who may have a considerable influence on trends because of their values, size or social media presence.

Visual Research

Design is a visual discipline that actively engages visual research to create design concepts, inspire ideas and solve problems. Images are used to document and produce visual records of different ways of seeing, understanding and analysing in an increasingly visual global culture. It also enables the study and use of images in broader contexts to communicate knowledge, experiences and ideas in ways that cannot be done using just words.

Designers undertake visual research as part of their creative journey, gathering visual images by using methods such as drawing, photography and moving image to identify areas of personal interest. Different kinds of visual research are gathered from different sources. **Primary research** involves gathering information that has not been collected before from original sources, such as a designer's own photographs, drawings or objects. **Secondary research** involves gathering information from existing sources such as articles in newspapers, popular magazines, books, journals and online sources.

To successfully create ideas and understand the context for design work, all designers need to carry out both primary and secondary research. When undertaking primary and secondary research there will be some immediate sources, for example museums, galleries and libraries. There will also be opportunities to visit special collections and archives and although these sorts of research visits take time to organize, they are extremely worthwhile. Local flea markets, vintage shops and army surplus outlets are also sources of research where individual or one-off items can be found. It is important to undertake this kind of object-based research where a three-dimensional object can be 'interrogated' rather than just seen as a digital image.

There are also numerous online sources that can be accessed by thousands, if not millions, of other people,

so it is important that they are credible, well-substantiated sources. Online research sources have global reach and have a place in building up a broad global knowledge. They may lead to the discovery of physical work that is in a specific gallery or related to a particular artist's work that may be on display.

Visual research should be approached as an ongoing process that is never completed and may inspire an immediate design brief or future briefs. To support this, a methodical and meticulous record of research, either physically in a sketchbook or digitally, should be kept.

All images are created to have a subtext (a meaning on several levels) and fashion images are no exception. In order to understand the meanings behind secondary source visual images, or the

Fashion images are a secondary source of visual research

Trend forecast magazine, View

reference they make to existing images and objects, it is important to be able to interpret them. Consider the following questions:

- What is the image of?
- What is its content?
- Who created it?
- When and why was it made?
- How do you read it?
- What will you do with it?

These questions can also be used to generate primary visuals and endow them with meanings so they can be interpreted on several levels.

Technical Research

Technical research should take the form of both primary investigation through deconstruction and testing out of ideas in three-dimensions, and secondary research, which could involve rediscovering traditional craft techniques, interviewing technical specialists or looking at competitor brands. Research to establish how a product will be used and its **ergonomics** (how well it sits on the body or performs for a particular function) is also vital. Sound technical research explains the processes and elements needed to make a product and helps build a personal catalogue of technical skills. Even if all of these skills are not mastered, detailed technical research means a designer at least understands how and when the skills are used most effectively in designing and manufacturing a product. Technical research should also be painstakingly recorded and can be captured through step-by-step photography and notes or moving images.

Consumer and Market Research

Increasingly, the idea of gender and age are becoming more complex areas through which to filter consumer behaviour. As societal shifts toward redefining traditional gendered roles have been broken down, strict product categories for men and women have given way to products that align more with attitudes or particular interests of consumer groups, for example sustainable, ethical products or functional products.

In the current landscape, it is important that a designer understands the lifestyle choices and attitudes of particular consumers or groups in order to reflect these requirements in a collection. Trends towards fitness and self-care have created functional, sporty and athleisure products (comfortable clothing and products for sports and everyday wear) made using light or **smart materials.** Smart materials are designed with properties that can be changed by factors such as light, heat or electrical impulses.

Acceleration of access to cheaper, more portable technology has resulted in new products for carrying smart gadgets around, obscuring the lines between work, home and leisure. Consumer focus groups, questionnaires, or online surveys on social media platforms can be used to conduct primary consumer and market research. This research can be used along with secondary sources, such as published reports on consumer behaviour and market trends, to design specific bags and accessories.

Shop research, whether online or in physical stores, helps analyse and evaluate other brands. It is useful to note what keeps consumers engaging with a competitor brand, the brand's design innovations and collaborations with other creatives, or their alignment with a particular societal issue.

Trend Research

Consumer behaviour is constantly shifting. Conducting trend research explains things currently shaping design and future directions. The job of a designer is a predictive one and expects insights into what might happen, as well as a strong understanding of what is currently happening. A valuable part of a designer's research is observing people, what they wear, where they shop and what they buy. This helps build a picture of different types of consumers and creates an understanding of how people dress from head-to-toe to reinforce the relationship between different clothing and accessories. People-watching also helps to spot and map new trends and styles of dress.

Understanding contemporary culture should go beyond a particular discipline, so research should exceed mainstream or niche fashion accessories brands to build knowledge of new trends in footwear, clothing, interior design, film, product design, music and literature. There are online trend services to support this, for example WGSN, who can provide a wealth of knowledge about global trends, giving a useful overview of new directions. It must be remembered, however, that these are general and widely accessible findings and should be used alongside personal interpretations of new trends based on your own research.

Producing a Concept

Once research is completed, organized into themes and edited, a concept takes shape. A concept must be original and lead to a collection that is worth making, as it is no longer possible to consider creative design without also considering sustainable approaches and environmental impacts. Designers need to examine the value of their concepts and if they will add to overconsumption and environmental damage.

Answering the following questions will help you to define a concept:

- What are the key themes within your concept?
- What does your brand stand for and what are its values?
- Who are your audiences and consumers?
- What informs your aesthetic?
- Does your brand serve a particular function?
- How have you considered the product life cycle and ways in which items can be sustainably produced or **recycled** at the end of life?
- What market level and price range are you aiming for?

Producing a mind map helps to answer these questions and to move forward with a concept that is broad enough to provide in-depth research to sustain a whole collection.

Concepts can be drawn directly from cultural or historical references or can come from more abstract ideas. The concept for a collection seeks to appeal to particular consumers or audiences. A strong concept is influenced by research and developmental processes but is separate from a brand's values. Brand values remain constant. For example, the commitment of

Stella McCartney (see pages 44–45) to sustainable design remains the same but her concepts change each season. A design concept can originate from an area of personal interest, a desire to solve a particular problem, like **zero-waste production**, or a brief set by a client or employer. No matter how a concept originates there are always restrictions within a brief to make sure the focus remains on what needs to be delivered as a final outcome. This outcome might involve the use of certain materials and techniques, the level of cost or the market level, but all will require slight differences in creative responses. Increasingly, brands are collaborating with other creative designers who may reinterpret a particular element of a brand, which then becomes the driving theme behind the whole new collection.

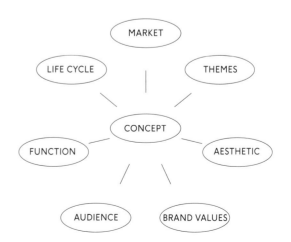

Opposite: Yohji Yamamoto for Y-3 in collaboration with adidas, A/W 2014/15

Design Development

The design development process starts with a summary of research, which is used to communicate the concept of a collection and generate initial design ideas. These initial ideas are then edited and developed into more finished designs.

Mood Boards

A **mood board** is a presentation of research edited into a visual summary of all the elements that make up a concept. It reflects the attitude of a collection and the specific design fundamentals used within it. A mood board defines inspirations, **colour palette** (the full range of colours used across a collection), materials, hardware, logo and other embellishments, and indicates the consumer or target audience, even giving some suggestion of consumer lifestyle. Through a montage of different images, a mood board presents a visual representation of an idea that will enable a design team, client or merchandiser to fully understand the concept and design narrative behind a collection.

A mood board can take a physical or digital format, although increasingly they are digital, which means they can be easily shared with creative teams. If a mood board is physical, it may take up a whole wall and can have the advantage of being a collaborative team effort. A physical mood board includes examples of fabric samples or actual pieces of hardware, while a digital board will rely on scans and creating information through two-dimensional images. It is important to remember that not all images have the same impact. Considering the number and impact of images, their scale and positioning, will create visual drama and emphasis.

An effective mood board includes enough images to communicate a concept clearly to others without the need to source more visuals. It should be able to answer any questions about the design intentions, signature silhouettes and techniques used, market context and consumer. A mood board that has been carefully designed to include these things may also include keywords that relate to a concept or a pen portrait of a consumer, but essentially a mood board should be a visual representation of the collection.

'Summer memories' fashion mood board

Ideas Generation

Research should inspire a strong concept, which in turn stimulates design ideas. Initially these ideas are generated through brainstorming multiple quick drawings, often recorded as small thumbnail sketches. Drawing starts the process of translating research into usable design ideas and is an important tool in design. Ideas can be recorded in a sketchbook or on loose sheets of paper. A sketchbook shows progression of ideas, while loose sheets allow all the ideas to be spread out and examined at once. As a sketchbook is compiled, a continuous process of editing happens, which generates ideas for colour, shape, texture, embellishment, construction and suggestions for hardware. A sketchbook is a working tool and a useful way to compile research and ideas into an ongoing library of creative responses, as well as a constant source of inspiration. It is essential to accurately record ideas, many of which will not go forward into a collection but may be revisited in future collections.

As designs progress, materials must be considered to see if they have the particular properties needed to be sympathetic to a design or technique. Environmental impact should also be considered at the initial design stage, along with design ideas for hardware and branding – both essential for fashion bags.

Once initial thumbnail sketches are produced, they will need to be edited so only the most promising ideas go forward for further development. Drawing becomes more and more refined with each stage of design development. Parts of the design will need to be explained in detail and drawn in 360 degrees, as a bag is a three-dimensional object with a base, sides and front, back and top views and an interior.

A designer needs to consider and explore the following three elements through drawing: how to build volume into a fashion bag so it can carry items; the ways in which the bag will close to prevent contents from spilling out and to keep items secure; and how the bag will be carried – whether on the shoulder, in the hand, across the body, or as a backpack.

Drawings should also be supported with trial samples, or **mock-ups**, of the three-dimensional elements of a bag to help resolve key design questions in a constant process between drawing and mocking up.

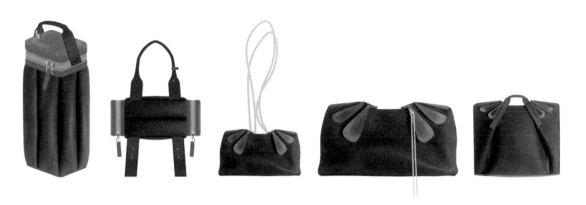

An example of an accessories line-up by Elleannor Moore

At this stage, ideas can be sketched out as line drawings or working drawings to literally work the product out. The key point is to convey a design idea clearly through drawn images. A brief will usually specify the number and type of products needed for the range, for example a tote, a crossbody bag, a backpack, etc. By producing a large quantity of developmental design drawings that explore possible permutations of style, scale and detailing, a focused collection of bags can then be selected. In addition to bags, small leather goods, such as purses, wallets, card holders, glasses cases and key fobs (see pages 148–51), will form part of the collection. These items need as much consideration in the design process as larger pieces in the range and often offer a way for a consumer to buy into a brand.

Presentation Sheets, Range Plans and Tech Packs

Analysing and editing skills are at the heart of the design cycle so only the most important and stimulating designs are taken forward. At this point enough design ideas must be generated to select from in order to create a balanced collection which reflects the wants and desires of consumers. A rigorous final editing of developmental design drawings should now take place and the final selection drawn up as design **presentation sheets**.

While the function of a mood board is to provide an edited brand narrative, the function of presentation sheets is to show a very detailed picture of each design, including all views necessary to explain the bag,

swatches of the materials it will be made in, as well as embellishments and hardware. Drawings are presented as rendered images of the final product that blend illustrations setting the mood of a collection with technical specifications explaining aspects of the design. The sheets need to be produced using a strong graphic format with a clear yet visually seductive layout and placement of images.

Larger companies will have a merchandising team to track individual styles of fashion bags from each collection or season and will advise designers on which styles have sold best, online or in store. Successful styles often stay in a collection but are reinvented through new materials, colourways or different hardware. The relationship between designers and merchandiser is key to making a successful range of fashion accessories, one balanced between creative design and commercial success.

Once the final designs have been selected and drawn as finished presentation sheets, it is useful to draw them as a line-up shown against the body. This assesses the balance of different sized bags in the collection. Each piece is then drawn up as part of a final **range plan** to make sure there are enough styles in the range to satisfy the original design brief.

A range plan includes information on the name of a style, the type of bag and construction, the colour palette, logos, all materials used and hardware, plus a small line drawing of each design with all product dimensions and the size and placement of each component. The range plan gives each style a number and wholesale and suggested retail prices.

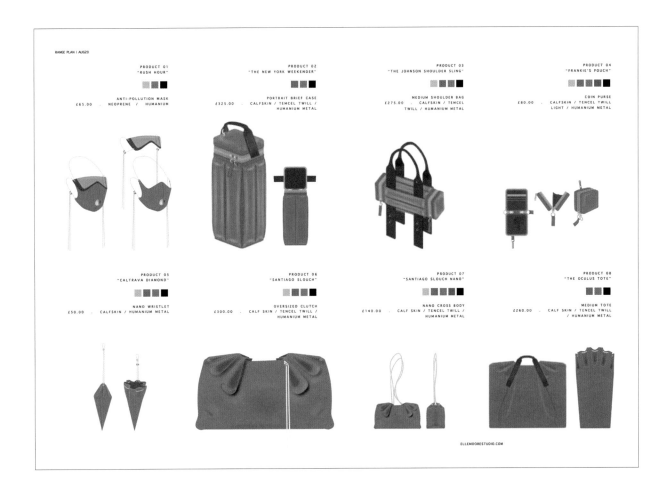

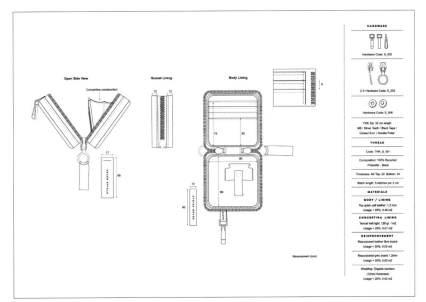

(Above) range plan and (left) technical drawing by Elleannor Moore

Bag created by Annika Andersson using virtual prototyping

Once the collection has been designed and drawn as a range plan, detailed technical packs are produced for each style. A **tech pack** is an essential document for designers and product developers. Product developers use tech packs to produce new collections by communicating exact standards of manufacture. The packs are multi-page documents which include the following: technical drawings, seam and stitch details, product dimensions, component information on every material used (including weight and finishes, colourways, embroideries and prints), components such as labels, zips, threads, trims, fastenings and embellishments, details of suppliers, delivery dates and packaging information. Tech packs can be used to give different manufacturers consistent technical information and ensure uniform standards of manufacture across different factories. The more precise the tech pack, the better the end result.

3D Virtual Prototyping

Some fashion brands have started to implement 3D virtual prototyping within their design and product development processes. Rather than producing tech packs, updating flat drawings or adjusting physical samples, 3D virtual prototyping offers brands the opportunity to use innovative technology to eliminate waste, lower their carbon footprint and be more cost effective.

3D virtual prototyping offers designers even greater creative freedom; the evolution of 3D modelling and material simulation has made it impossible to distinguish physical products from digital ones. Results can be achieved rapidly so designers can accurately see what a design will look like in 360 degrees without having to make it. When this technology incorporates features that can translate a virtual prototype into physical reality, designs can be uniformly and accurately communicated to all departments within a company, manufacturers and retailers.

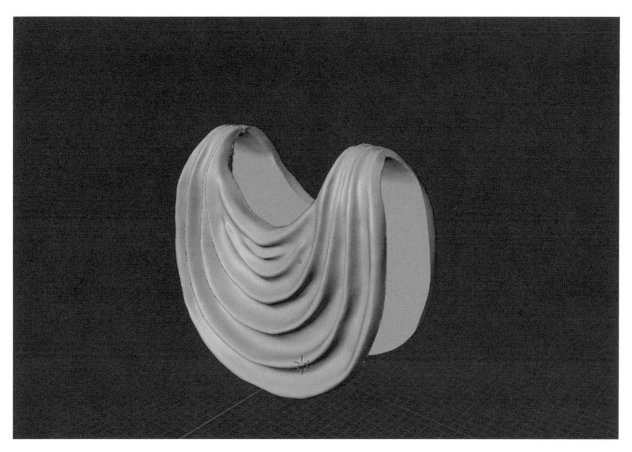

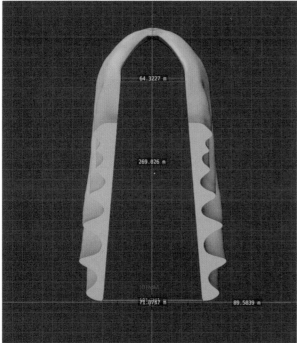

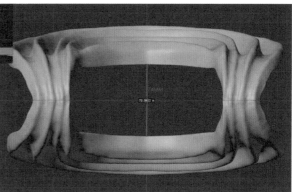

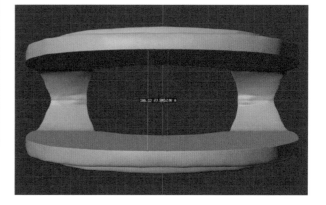

Virtual prototyping by Serena Bashir
using Rhino

Design Considerations

Increasingly, consumers are becoming more aware of, and concerned by, the conditions under which fashion products are designed and manufactured, and what happens to them at the end of their useful lives. Designers need to consider not only sustainable design and manufacture, but also ethical and socially just practices so that items can be manufactured without exploitation and have the ability to be repaired, repurposed or recycled.

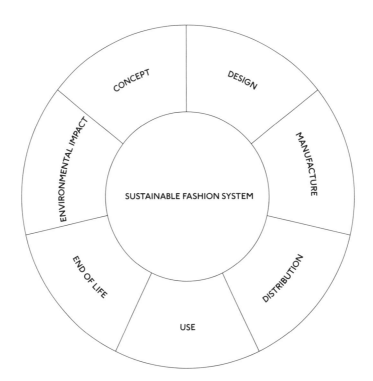

Sustainable Design

Sustainable design is an approach that creates a product that considers its environmental, social and economic impacts, from the initial research and design phase through to the end of its life. Sustainable design meets our current needs without having a damaging impact on outcomes for future generations. In response to the global environmental crisis we are facing, it is no longer a fringe activity of mainstream design. Sustainable design thinking empowers designers to explore more **regenerative design** solutions that restore or revitalize, demonstrating that all areas of design and market levels can benefit from sustainable solutions.

JW Pei Eva shoulder bag in vegan leather with 100 per cent recycled plastic lining

There are varied approaches to sustainable design so individual designers need to define for themselves how to integrate sustainable practice into their creative process. This could be through exploring the use of more environmentally-friendly materials, heritage and craft-creating designs that have longevity, human-centred design that solves a particular problem, or **design for disassembly** to create products that are easier to recycle.

Through a more considered approach to design, a balance between environmental and economic factors can be found to formulate future design concepts. For fashion accessories, improvements are happening in leather tanning processes (see page 100) and in the production of materials such as denim, which have historically had a high environmental impact due to their use of vast quantities of water.

The ability to recycle a product and convert it into a new material or object is becoming one of the most important factors to consider when designing. Most bags are made of several different materials and by minimizing the use of glues, or changing the mix of materials and hardware, a product becomes far more recyclable, reducing its environmental impact.

All designers need to think about the product throughout its life cycle and what happens to it at the end of its life. Answering the following questions will help do this:

- Does the design have a purpose?
- Does the design have longevity?
- Can the product's components be replaced or repaired?
- Can the product be made from materials that are biodegradable, recyclable, or regenerative?
- Can the product be manufactured with the minimum impact on the environment?

To develop innovative and original sustainable design solutions, specific research is needed to build a picture of new innovations and interventions in the field.

Brand Identity

Brand identity is an imperative for a fashion brand. Brands seek to have a consistent and easily understood brand message, which is reflected in their products. The identity of a brand consists of elements that make a brand recognizable, communicated through its products, key colour stories,

Adidas instantly recognizable three stripes

Seasonality

Seasonality is something that may be more or less important to individual brands and is communicated to designers through the brief. The idea of seasonality is becoming a contentious area for some contemporary designers. Traditionally, spring/summer and autumn/winter collections were delineated by colour and purpose. Collections are presented at biannual global trade shows six months in advance of a season. Summer collections generally favour lighter colours, and winter collections darker shades. A variety of bags, such as beach bags and luggage, produced in the summer season focus on holiday travel and use for outdoor activities. These use lighter materials, such as raffia, straw and nylon, and waterproof materials, along with a lighter palette to fit into the 'resort-wear' product category. There are new product categories, for example the highly functional athleisure and festival-wear categories, that may be marketed with a strong seasonal bias but are in fact available all year round. Undoubtedly there are different types of bags used during different seasons, but the product categories reflect a blurring of lines between the very seasonal collections in favour of collections that reflect activities.

Some designers, like Michael Kors and Tommy Hilfiger, have added in more seasons, while other designers prefer to produce seasonless ranges of accessories where the driving factor behind new purchases may be function rather than style, colour and materials. The trend toward 'buy-now-wear-now' has also speeded up the process of bringing a new product to market and fuelled a demand for immediacy in the minds of consumers. Although compressing the timeline between seeing a product on the catwalk and being able to buy it has been challenging for brands and retailers, it has placed purchasing power in the hands of the consumer. Some brands, such as Burberry, have pioneered

graphics, logos, fonts, promotional material, events, advertising and social media, and through the icons chosen to represent it. In order to develop into a well-executed collection, which enhances the history and heritage of a brand or creates a new one, a designer needs to understand how far to deviate from the existing position of a brand to move it forward.

Each component that contributes to the brand identity and image must be understood and considered during the design process. There are numerous techniques for applying branding to a product, for example the printed double FF Fendi canvas or the Prada triangular logo plate. Fashion brands rely on branding to convey their heritage and cultural experience through their logos and also through bespoke hardware such as charms, logo plates and details.

immediate delivery where they are able to sell more products, so seasonality as we have known it will continue to shift.

Price Range

The **price range** of a collection reflects the individual price for each item from the most expensive to the cheapest and forms an integral part of the brief. It is vital a designer understands the production price of a fashion bag and how small changes in a design can raise or lower production prices. The price of the product will determine the quality of manufacture, the types of materials and quality of hardware used, design styles and details, application of logos, the way in which the product is communicated through social media channels, the types of brand icons who will be aligned with the product, and even the experience of buying it. The price will also create a set of expectations for consumers about the differences between expensive and cheaper products. Higher-priced designer collections are expected to be more revolutionary, with new styles emerging, which then trickle down to the lower end of the market. However, this is not always the case. The idea of limited-edition styles originated in the high street but has been adopted by designer brands. These brands introduce a few pieces into a range for a short period of time followed by a wider online release and often in collaboration with other creatives. This has fuelled an enormous second market for the sale of limited-edition products.

Tommy Hilfiger catwalk collection, S/S 2017

Supreme's red product range

Colour

'Colour is the mother tongue of the subconscious.'
Carl Jung, psychoanalyst

Every day we make choices by putting different colours together. From the moment we pick out our clothes each morning we use colour to convey our identity and our emotions.

As our moods fluctuate, we know that colour plays a role in informing our attitudes. Colour is often the first thing we notice, and it symbolizes different things in different cultural contexts, triggering responses at a subconscious level. The colour red, for example, is associated with anger, love, ambition, danger or good fortune, depending on your cultural perspective.

When colours are contrasted, we perceive a visual mix; this mix will depend on the proportions of each of the colours used, so not only is the colour significant but also the proportions it is used in. The intensity of the colours will also determine how a product looks.

The way in which a brand or designer uses colour is not accidental; every aspect of a colour palette has been carefully considered, researched and analysed. Colour has become integral to brand communication, translated into logos, packaging and advertisements, or through carefully worked out colour stories to convey the seasonality and mood in a collection. For some brands colour is so important they have trademarked a particular shade, for example the red used on the soles of Christian Louboutin shoes and the blue used by Tiffany.

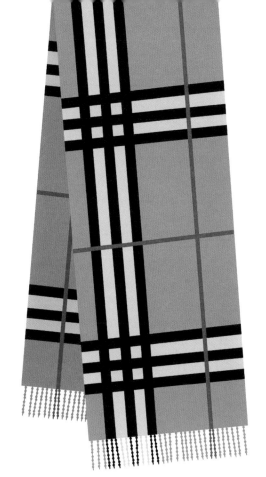

Burberry's iconic check

Colour stories are usually linked to the concept or theme of a collection, derived from images, photographs, drawings or paintings, or even objects like a piece of china, a shell or a textile. A particular season or a place can also inspire a colour palette. Colours can be extracted from the source of inspiration and refined down through experimentation with proportion, **hue** and **tone** to construct a colour palette of **base colours** used in larger quantities and **accent colours** used sparingly to add flavour and focus in a range. Historically, companies have matched their colour palettes to particular colour systems like Pantone, which is a global system used to match and communicate standardized colours across manufacturers in different countries. Colour trends are created eighteen months to two years in advance of the market by colour trend forecasters and are given names within a collection to identify them. Some companies have the technology, or are of a sufficient size, to create their own colours, developing specific shades that may reflect aspects of colour trends but are essentially unique to them.

Within the industry seasonal colour trends are created to keep up with consumer expectations. Michael Kors created two new additional seasons – Resort in spring/summer and Pre-Fall in autumn/winter – to create more colour choices for its customers.

Colour is an inexpensive way for a brand to create an impact. A designer must understand colour in a global context and achieve a balance of accent colours and darker tones in a colour palette that makes it look fresh and new. Once the palette is finalized it needs to be applied within a range of fashion accessories in a cohesive way by correctly identifying the opportunities to use colour in an accessory. For example, colour can be used to emphasize areas such as linings, contrast top stitching, zips and zip pulls, as well as the main body of a bag.

Materials

A designer needs to be familiar with all the different types of materials used in a product and understand their qualities so that the right material for a particular design is selected. All materials have sets of characteristics that make them more or less suitable for solid fashion bags that need to maintain a structure or for bags that are soft, tactile and unstructured. In terms of accessories, the material a bag is made from is important because of the weight of the product, which will become heavier when in use. The density of materials, therefore, needs to be considered, along with how well a particular product wears. If a fabric lining in a leather bag wears out, the bag becomes useless, while the body of the bag is still usable. In addition to this there are unseen materials, such as reinforcements, used to support the body of a bag or strengthen certain areas. These materials must be selected with care and knowledge of how they will perform in relation to the main materials used in a product.

Materials can be sourced through commercial trade shows, like Première Vision and Lineapelle that take place twice a year, or directly from tanneries and merchants. Brands can become synonymous with particular materials, like the nylon used by Prada, or work with manufacturers and tanneries to create innovative new materials. Leather, which is considered a by-product of the meat industry, is still the predominant material used in fashion bags, but when approaching materials choices designers now need to consider sustainable production and sourcing of materials, including alternatives to leather, due to growing consumer interest in non-leather bags.

The basic principles of working in leather are to understand the size and quality of the skin being used and its unique qualities of structure and finish (see pages 100–2). Some synthetic fabrics may be more environmentally damaging than leather but there are natural leather-effect alternatives made from fruit, mushrooms, coconuts, paper and cactuses which are now readily available (see pages 103–13).

Hardware

Hardware, the metal elements on a bag, has practical functions, for example to attach handles and close or protect areas. It can also be used to create a strong, instantly recognizable design handwriting, which is an indispensable part of a fashion bag. Hardware can make functional details become part of the aesthetic of the bag simply by changing their scale, application and position.

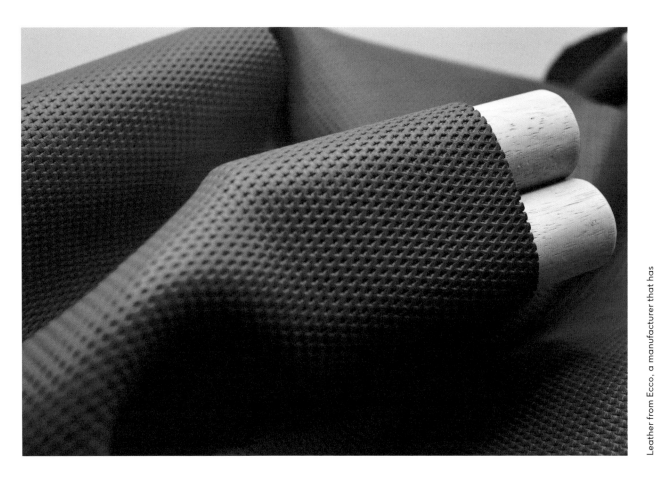

Leather from Ecco, a manufacturer that has pioneered better production methods

A fashion bag is a three-dimensional object, and this creates an opportunity for a designer to consider how hardware can become an integral part of the design aesthetic used over several collections. Hardware presents a design and branding opportunity on a fashion bag, but it can be expensive to originate new styles. There is a certain amount of 'off-the-shelf' hardware available, but this may not be of the necessary quality and colour, or the right size and style, and may not be consistently available. As the costs of creating new hardware are significant, only established brands are able to make the investment in their own hardware. Smaller brands, who use existing hardware, should source their hardware before designing products, as rings, clips, buckles, zips, zip pulls, and studs all come in standard sizes and

need to fit the dimensions of straps or fastenings on a bag. The number of styles of hardware used across a collection can be kept to a minimum so the same components can be used multiple times. The application of the logo, which can be stamped into hardware, can be made more cost effective by incorporating logos into the initial tool and mould costs.

Mulberry textured leather clutch bag with gold chain handle and gold twist-lock fastening

3
Drawing

The physical act of drawing creates a sensory experience that engages creative thinking, exploration and problem solving. It encourages conversations about the potential direction, execution and possibilities of an idea. The more you draw, the more confident you become, and you soon start drawing without thinking about it. Everything you draw should be preserved and should not be edited, so it can be revisited. Drawing can be done by hand or digitally.

Hand Drawing and Computer Drawing

Hand drawing is the fastest, most efficient way to record thoughts and to work through ideas. It is easy to see the development stages of an idea through hand drawing rather than the process of reworking ideas on a computer screen or tablet. Hand drawing helps resolve complex shapes and is an excellent way to work through and communicate ideas, particularly at an initial stage. It also allows an idea to be shared and discussed at a conceptual level.

In the age of digital imagery, it is tempting to dismiss hand drawing as outdated, but there is a subtlety and sophistication that mark making on paper conveys. The nuances of a drawn design idea are not always apparent in a digital image. In front of a screen it is easy to fast track to final outcomes and miss out on the accidents and creative risk taking that lead to unexpected results. The steps from creative thinking to a drawn idea are invaluable for designers and without this we may be de-skilling ourselves in a rush to produce everything digitally.

While some designers may be less creative in front of a computer screen, computer-aided design (CAD) drawings have an important place within the industry as they provide a consistency that hand drawing cannot. Initially, working directly onto a computer screen to create images can be time-consuming and does not allow a designer to connect to a drawing in the same way as freehand sketching. CAD drawings are, however, effective at creating permutations of a design, using different proportions, adding logos, colour and texture to make realistic design renderings. They produce professional, readable and accurate technical drawings (see page 72), templates for portfolio pages (see page 173–82) and range plans (see page 54).

Graphic tablets that convert hand drawing directly to a digital image on screen provide the best of freehand drawing and CAD drawing. They consist of a flat pad and an electronic pen to accurately capture natural hand movements, producing more complex shapes and smoother curves, and offering a quick and more intuitive way to work. They are also compatible with other industry standard CAD software.

The greatest revolution in image generation has come through 3D visualization systems, which have been standard practice within architecture, vehicle design and product design for many years. The fast-paced nature of fashion has made the industry slow to incorporate new technology, so many companies still use hand drawing and **rendering** (colouring) using 2D CAD illustration software. Fashion bags and footwear, which incorporate elements of both product design and fashion, have been quicker to adopt 3D visualization, modelling and prototyping systems for design and component making. Material simulation is now so advanced that technology has reached a tipping point where the process of sketching and rendering design ideas may be changed significantly.

Drawing for the Design Process

There are four phases of drawing that support the design process: ideation drawings, process sketches, persuasive illustrations and technical drawings. Each phase requires different styles of drawing and different drawing tools. The phases are interconnected and allow a designer to move from an initial sketched idea to a final rendered image of a product. It is important to understand the difference between drawings that support each stage of the design process. Each different phase of drawing needs to be mastered using a combination of hand drawing and CAD drawing and, increasingly, 3D visualization software.

Whether hand drawing or drawing using a computer, the first thing to establish is the type of drawing you want to do and then decide on the medium you wish to use to produce it.

Phase One: Ideation Drawings

Ideation drawings are quick, small sketches used to capture ideas rapidly once a concept is chosen and should facilitate ways to draw a large number of initial responses to a brief. Most designers will use hand drawing during this brainstorming phase, using graphite or mechanical pencils to record ideas in a sketchbook or on a sheet of paper. Drawing with a pencil feels natural, as if the pencil is an extension of the hand, and allows for quick outlines or construction lines to be captured. Initial sketches of first ideas are usually drawn as basic front and back views not using perspective. They lack detail but help define signature silhouettes and proportions for a collection. These sketches are generally drawn using a range of different pencils or black fineliner pens, without colour being

applied to them. Quick sketching during this phase produces small thumbnail drawings fitting several images onto one page. Hand drawing can be most useful to generate a flow of ideas, which can then be edited and worked out as more considered designs during phase two.

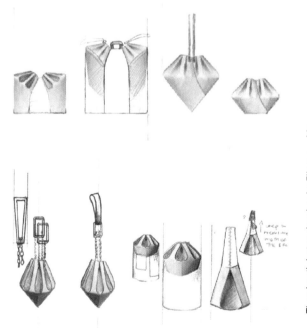

Thumbnail design sketches by Elleannor Moore

69

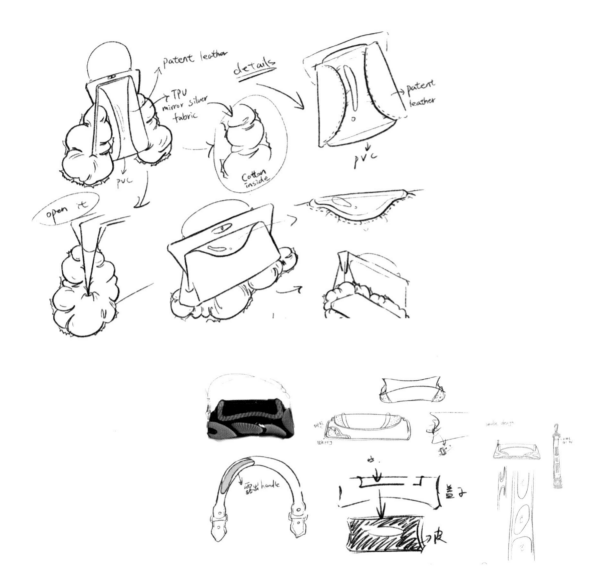

Sketching to explain a design by Zuxin Qiu

Phase Two: Process Sketches

In phase two **process sketches**, or working drawings, are usually hand-drawn sketches used to interrogate ideas and solve design problems. After editing ideation drawings to unearth the most promising design ideas, working drawings are used to develop the ideas in more detail and to record design thinking based on knowledge of prototyping and construction. During phase two, creative ideas are usually drawn in perspective as line drawings and tempered with the reality of manufacturing requirements. These drawings represent design thinking drawn out in stages. They may be sketches of a whole product or part of an accessory and include **expanded views** of sections and details like hardware. Particularly successful designs can be picked out in a colour or partly rendered to draw attention to them on the page. Usually presented as shaded line drawings, these process sketches work out and explain a product to the point where it can be mocked up in three-dimensions and refined through further sketches drawn from the three-dimensional mock-ups. Once designs have been 'worked out' through drawing they can be edited to be drawn up as illustrations on a presentation board in phase three.

Technical drawings by Zuxin Qiu

Phase Three: Persuasive Illustrations

During this phase of the design cycle, designs will be drawn as finished drawings that will be coloured. At this point, drawings presented as illustrations are at their most useful because they will sell the concept, tone and mood of the collection by persuading others to support the design ideas. Illustrations are not drawn to scale and may not include all the detail of a working drawing. Reflecting the personal style and flair of an individual designer's drawing skill, they are indicative and not representative of products.

Once sketches have been completed, colour is applied to the illustration. Hand rendering is time-consuming, but can be achieved using coloured pencils, paints or marker pens. Marker pens are most commonly used in design studios because they are quick and easy and can be applied to give a flat, even colour and finish. Most rendering is done using CAD illustration software, applying different textures and variations of colour which previously have always been done by hand. Digital images have the advantage of being easily edited, recoloured or altered, but the disadvantage of appearing like generic images which use the same software and toolboxes. Hand-drawn line illustrations can be scanned into a computer and then rendered, or even partly coloured, and then scanned and coloured to produce more individual results.

71

Technical drawings by Zuxin Qiu

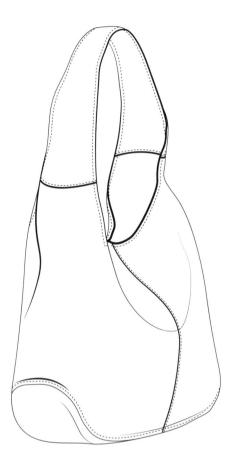

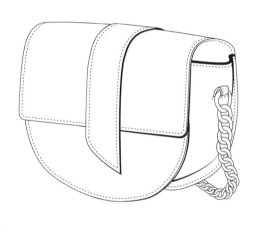

Phase Four: Technical Drawings

In the last phase of drawing, the aim is to achieve uniformity through clear, precise line drawings communicating technical information in order to recreate a product exactly by explaining structure and function. These drawings are used to create tech packs (see pages 54–6), which are essential in the making of initial samples. The most valuable tools for this stage produce flat CAD **technical drawings** that are clearer and more precise than hand-drawn technical drawings and communicate how a product functions or is made. These types of CAD drawings can be scaled and include stitch details, zips, zip pulls, D rings, eyelets and buckles. A lot of skill is required to draw bag shapes, some of which will be soft or more constructed, and also the components being used.

Increasingly, these sorts of visualizations are now being done using 3D realization tools, not simply to create a technical drawing accurately but also a fully rendered three-dimensional **prototype**. This prototype provides other members of a design team, merchandisers and manufacturers with product information that far exceeds the most detailed tech pack.

73

Drawing on the Page

The appeal of sketching is not just the drawing but also the position of drawings on a page or screen. Positioning can make drawings more or less interesting, readable or noticeable. A designer's ambition is always to communicate ideas effectively, so placement of images on the pages must be kept in mind. A focal point for a page should be established during each phase of drawing. This is as true for sketchbook pages as it is for more formal presentations and portfolio pages, although the focal point for each page of drawing will be expressed differently. Hand-drawn or computer-generated images can be placed symmetrically on the page, or asymmetrically to add more drama, emphasis and direction, to focus the eye across the page or from top to bottom of the screen. The scale of each drawing also has an impact. A series of small thumbnails conveys something different to a single large illustration, but each phase of drawing will have a 'visual hierarchy'. Overcrowding a page with drawings can lose focus and too few drawings on a page can make design ideas look weak. Drawing a few thumbnails or working drawings in a contrasting colour on a page automatically draws attention to them; they can also be partly rendered or circled. A change of scale can be used to show the importance of an expanded view or of a component. A single rendered illustration can add power to a presentation.

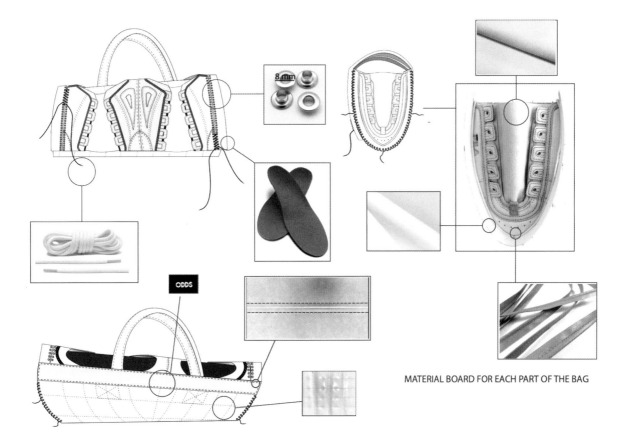

MATERIAL BOARD FOR EACH PART OF THE BAG

Material board by Sebastian Mendoza Gutierrez

For each phase of drawing, the placement of images on the page needs to be carefully considered. During the ideation and process drawing phases, drawings can be done in a physical sketchbook. A convenient size of sketchbook is A5 (half letter) or A4 (letter), both of which can be easily carried around. Drawing on one side of a page, or drawing across two pages to create an A3 (tabloid) page, should also be considered. Making a rough page template helps technical drawing look consistent and clear. Each image can be drawn within the same width of the border on a page and expanded views can be drawn to show individual components of a design and positioned in the same place on each sheet. Persuasive illustration requires the most consideration as these drawings are predominantly used for presentations and need to be dynamic and impactful in their location on the page.

Hand drawing allows for a degree of control over the composition on a page and where each drawing is placed, which determines how a design is read. It can be quite time-consuming, however, to place images and manipulate them to remove backgrounds, rescale or reposition them on a computer screen.

Drawing Bags

Accessories designers face many of the same drawing challenges as product designers. Studying the way product designers draw basic shapes, components, or expanded views of layers of detail is a useful exercise to understand how to draw particular areas of bags and to explain ideas through detailed sketching. Essentially, bags are drawn in several different views or planes to provide all the information to comprehend them as three-dimensional objects. Views can be of the front, back, top, bottom, side or three-quarters, the latter providing the most information in one drawing. To draw a bag as a convincing object, a designer needs to understand perspective drawing and master three-quarter views. Once able to draw a freehand perspective view of a bag, it is much easier to understand how to draw bags using CAD software or sketching apps to generate different views and rendering.

Perspective Drawing

In order to create realistic drawings, it is important to know what perspective is and how and when to use it. **Perspective drawings** show spatial depth and are the most realistic way to represent three-dimensional objects on a two-dimensional surface in order to give accurate information about their dimensions of height, width and depth, and their position in relation to each other. It can also be used for drawing components and details and working out the many facets of a product. Successful perspective drawing looks natural and presents objects as they would be seen by the human eye.

All perspective drawings have a **vanishing point**, which helps a designer to accurately show depth in three-dimensional spaces. Vanishing points, the furthest points away from the viewer of an image, are the spots where lines converge allowing a feeling of depth to be created. There are several different types of perspective drawing: **one-point** perspective, where all lines converge to a single point; **two-point** perspective, where horizontal lines converge to two points; and **three-point** perspective, where there are three points of convergence. Two- and three-point perspectives are most useful for drawing fashion bags to show three-quarter views, providing the most information about the design.

Many CAD programs have filters that create perspective-correct images to translate drawings into digital representations. Devices such as 3D printers can interpret these drawings of whole products or components during the manufacturing stage.

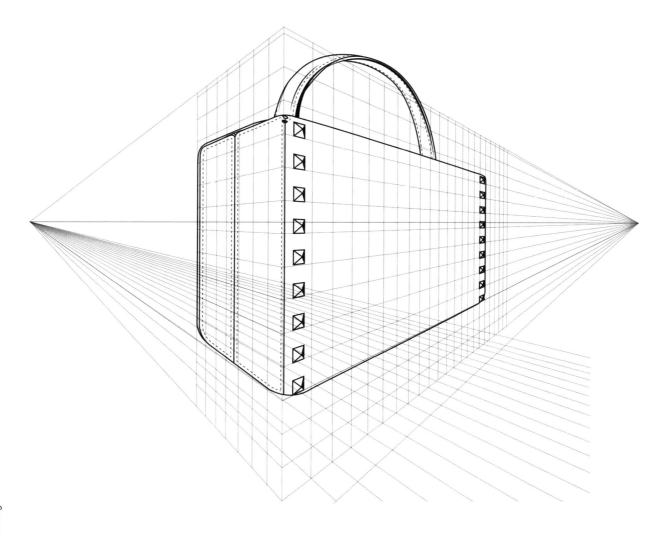

Perspective drawing of a bag

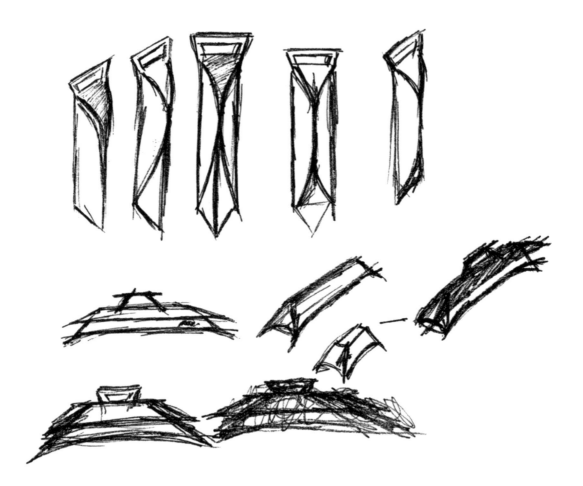

Example of line and shading thumbnail drawings by Maxim Winckers

Line and Shading

Along with perspective drawing, types of line should be considered; different thicknesses or changes in colours of line can alter the emphasis of a drawing, creating depth and dimension. Lines are used to outline a whole drawing or a section, along with cross-hatching to create shading. Learning to draw basic geometric shapes, such as pyramids, spheres, cubes, cylinders, squares, triangles, rectangles and ovals, will help in illustrating more difficult and irregular shapes of soft or hard bags. Even the most complex shapes can be broken down into simpler shapes that are a combination of geometric forms.

Once these simple shapes are mastered, it is important to learn how to apply shading to show the different areas where light hits an object. Before creating shading, it is crucial to choose the direction of the light source in a drawing so that shading can be used to create an illusion of depth. Effective shading is a way to add detail to design drawings that is not always obvious from drawn outlines. With practice, shading can become an instinctive part of the drawing process. Shading is particularly important when trying to convey the volume of a bag or drawing hardware.

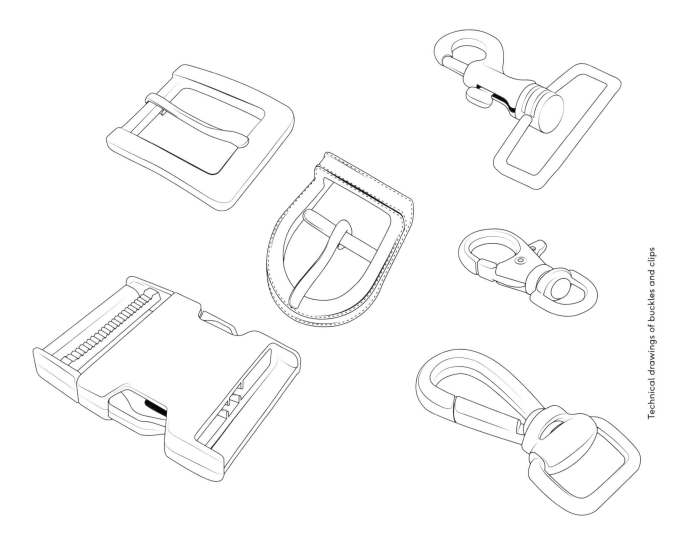

Technical drawings of buckles and clips

Once basic construction lines are in place, shading can be added within the outlines of a shape. Shading diagonally to construction lines creates more depth and interest in the drawing. Realistic shading includes dark, medium and light tones, which can be achieved by shading over an area several times, applying more pressure when drawing, or by using cross-hatching. Darker shaded tones are used on areas that receive the least amount of light and can be used to emphasize areas of a design drawing.

The same process of using geometric shapes can be used for drawing components like chains or the teeth of a zip. When drawing freehand ideas for components, such as buckles or D rings, there is a misconception that a precise idea of the finished object is needed, when in fact a rough shape can be developed into a more finished design. Observational drawings of existing components can be used to build drawing skills. Existing components, such as buckles, chains, D rings and zips, can be scanned and imported into CAD software like Adobe illustrator, or 3D visualization software, and manipulated to develop new components.

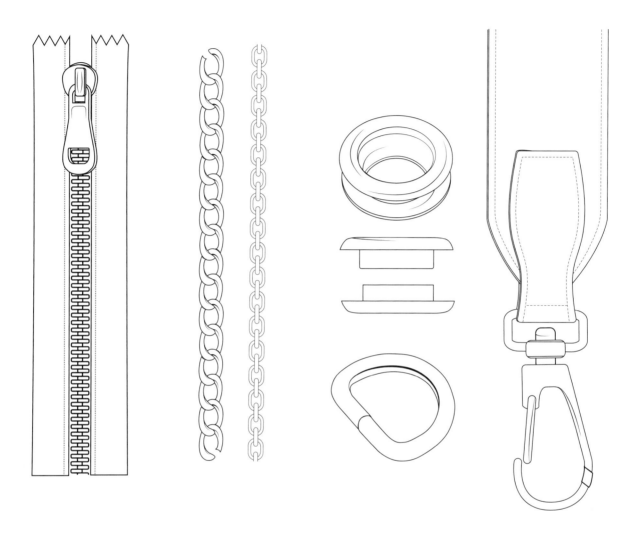

Technical drawings of fashion bag hardware:
zip, chains, eyelet, D ring and buckle with clip

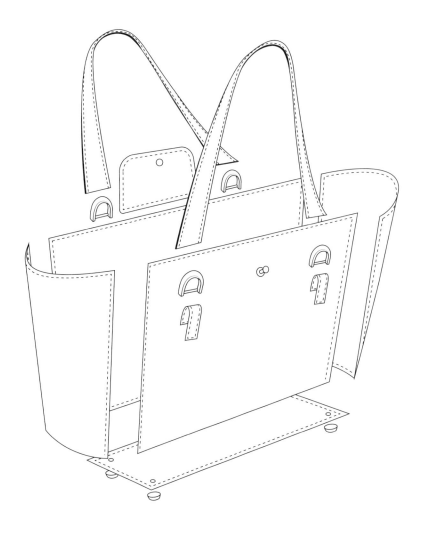

Expanded view of a bag

Expanded Views

A drawing of an expanded view is a way to disassemble a product through layers of drawing in order to show its component parts, separated out by small distances between each layer. An expanded view explains how a product is constructed or fits together and is drawn as a three-dimensional sketch. Expanded views are commonly used during the process sketching phase and presented as working drawings, which help to problem solve. They are also used extensively in tech packs to explain exactly how something is constructed. The projection of expanded views can be drawn from above on a diagonal and requires a considerable amount of practice before it is mastered.

There are several image manipulation computer packages that are excellent for producing expanded views of products. These can be used in conjunction with hand-drawn images, which can be scanned and imported into a computer program and used as a template for other designs. Basic construction lines can be neatened, and the image can be rendered.

Hand drawing, computer drawing, and 3D visualization and image manipulation are now interconnected processes that designers need to understand. They also need to know when to apply these different ways of creating images.

The Hand Drawing Toolbox

Freehand drawing is about learning to master creative and expressive drawings that accurately communicate design intentions. The best way to become confident in hand drawing is to draw from objects. This kind of observational drawing will help to develop a personal style and a catalogue of your own 'shorthand' methods of drawing bag shapes, components such as chains, buckles, zips or stitching, and textures of materials or leather. By drawing bags from different angles you will understand different perspectives and gain confidence in drawing a three-dimensional object from an idea. Practising drawing different bags helps build both a comprehensive understanding of range building and of developmental sketching to change proportion, size and details.

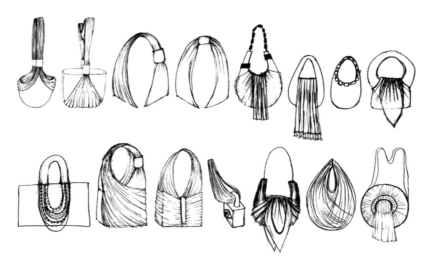

Thumbnail showing different proportions and designs of a bag by Serena Bashir

It is advisable to experiment with different ways of mark making to find the right tools. Hard and soft pencils, Copic, Prismacolor, Letraset or Pantone markers, along with fineliner and ballpoint pens, are good to use in developing freehand drawing skills and are easily portable. Watercolour, gouache, acrylic paints and inks take more practise and are less portable. Drawing on paper offers an opportunity to experiment with different textures and colours of paper or to use collages of different drawings together on one page. Once a personal style develops it will suit specific media. Experimenting with different media will help you to discover techniques that can be replicated using CAD software.

The Digital Toolbox

CAD software for illustration uses a computer to create, modify or analyse design drawings. The advances in CAD software have made it possible to recreate every technique used in hand drawing. Creating designs based on geometric shapes, technical two-dimensional drawings, three-dimensional perspective drawings and expanded views, image manipulation, animations or 3D prototyping are all possible using the software.

There are two main categories of 3D design software: CAD software for creative design and CAD 3D modelling and visualization software to create objects, such as bag prototypes or component parts of a bag, as screen-rendered 3D models which can then be 3D printed as functional objects.

There are numerous software packages available, with some larger fashion brands developing their own software. Some of the most common software packages suitable for beginners or more advanced designers are listed below. Some licensed CAD packages can be expensive, but increasingly there are free or open-source apps and software that are comparable with licensed products. As with hand drawing, becoming proficient in different CAD software takes time and effort.

CAD for Creative Design

Adobe Creative Suite is a comprehensive toolbox which has the advantage of containing all the tools needed by contemporary designers in one package. It includes Illustrator, Photoshop, InDesign and Premiere Pro, which cover all facets of design from drawing, rendering and logo ideation to video editing. It is the most utilized CAD software in the fashion industry.

Illustrator and Photoshop are used to access the drawing tools needed to turn simple shapes and colours into more sophisticated designs, as well as for photo editing, compositing, and digital painting. InDesign is a desktop publishing and typesetting software application used for creating presentations, portfolio pages and lookbooks. Premiere Pro is the industry-leading video editing software used to craft moving images into finished films and videos.

Free, open-source or lower-priced software usually includes some of the tools in Adobe Creative Suite. Pixlr is free CAD software for photo editing and image manipulation. It has an extensive toolbox with over 600 effects, useful for rendering and manipulating images. Inkscape creates intricate and detailed visuals and supports advanced features of blending and cloning objects, creating variation and development of designs. Scribus is a cheap software used as an alternative to InDesign and offers professional page layout programs and a range of drawing tools. DaVinci Resolve is a free video editing tool, with impressive colour correction features, that has become an industry standard.

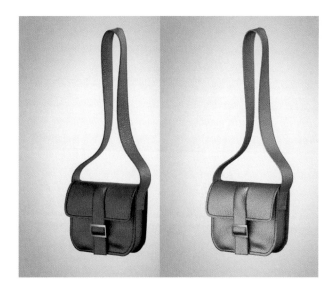

CAD drawings of a crossbody bag in different colourways by Annika Andersson

CAD for 3D Modelling

3D CAD software for modelling has specific uses as a technical tool, with functions such as advanced rendering and animation to better visualize products. Increasingly, designers with this kind of specialist knowledge and proficiency are being recruited into companies to fulfil roles as digital designers.

Tinkercad is a free online 3D design app geared towards beginners or those with no experience of 3D modelling. It uses an intuitive block-building concept, allowing designers to develop models from a set of basic shapes. The online software comes with a library of files that can be used to find suitable shapes and manipulate them as desired so they can be 3D printed.

AutoCAD is a well-established CAD software that has the advantage of being both a 2D CAD software and a 3D modelling program. This software facilitates two-dimensional design drawing and three-dimensional models that can be readily converted to files for 3D printing.

Rhino is a market leader and considered to be the most versatile 3D modelling system. It is a commercial 3D CAD software program used extensively in the industry. The program allows points and shapes to be manipulated in numerous different ways to build a wide range of printable objects and components. Rhino's strongest feature is its versatility in creating complex three-dimensional models.

CLO3D is a fashion design and 3D visualization software to develop 'true-to-life' three-dimensional garments, fashion accessories and footwear. CLO3D has drastically reduced the time it takes to create patterns, products and components. It also enables them to be rendered quickly using a library of different materials, including leather, to create images that are hard to distinguish from physical products. The advantage of CLO3D is its speed, as adjustments take minutes, and it has applications within the fashion industry that go beyond the design development phase.

Blender 3D is the free, open-source professional 3D package developed by the Blender Foundation, a non-profit organization. Blender 3D supports the entire 3D pipeline, from computer graphics, 3D printed modelling and rendering to texturing and animation. Blender is accessible and valuable for a wide range of users.

4
Materials

Now more than ever, at this time of climate crisis, the materials used in fashion need careful consideration. Pure aesthetics can no longer dictate the choice, nor is it enough to use 'sustainable materials' in a broad and superficial way. Increasingly, consumers want a guarantee of the provenance of the products they buy. Building a thoughtful approach to sustainability that can be integrated into the design and manufacturing process is essential to making the supply chain more transparent and creating lasting changes. Brands are responding to shifting consumer trends towards greener, eco-friendly materials. So as well as the obvious aesthetic factors, such as finish, colour and texture, environmental impact and **biodegradability** (the ability to be broken down into organic material) should be considered when selecting materials.

Lightweight nylons, polyurethane or PU (a synthetic plastic material), and cotton canvas remain the most popular alternatives to leather for fashion bags and accessories, but this is an area of innovation and new materials are being developed all the time that utilize waste products from different industries.

Main Materials for Bags

Bags are made from a wide range of textiles, from traditional leather to fabrics such as cotton, canvas, denim, wool and hemp. They are also made from materials such as cork, raffia and metal, and from synthetic plastics (PVC, polypropylene, nylon) or acrylic. Plastic and acrylic textiles are man-made through a process of chemical synthesis, as opposed to natural fibres that are directly derived from living organisms.

The choice of materials often rests on the requirements of an individual design, ease of manufacture, cost and the aesthetics of the day. Each material has advantages and disadvantages. Each material also has an environmental impact.

Leather

The leather industry is one of the oldest industries in the world and has become a huge global economy. Historically, leather has been the material of choice for fashion bags and accessories due to its unique properties of breathability, durability and flexibility, as well as its suitability for different types of bag. Its status as a luxury material is synonymous with heritage, craftsmanship and quality.

While the demand for leather goods continues to increase, so too does criticism of the environmental impact of the **tanning** process used during leather production. This criticism is generating environmentally-friendly and sustainable design solutions and a desire by many designers to address these issues at the design stage.

Essentially, the leather industry recycles leather waste by-products from the meat and agriculture industries that would otherwise be burnt or sent to landfill. The commercial tanning process, which converts animal skins into leather, uses polluting chemicals to stop leather hides from decomposing and to give them a supple, colour-fast finish. It is the most environmentally damaging phase in leather processing. Legislation controlling global production of leather introduced in the early 2020s, means tanneries are now expected to meet higher standards of production to address concerns of working conditions, animal welfare, deforestation, water overuse, and emissions that contribute to climate change. New technology and machinery have been developed to improve leather production and create a transparent supply chain so that examples of best practices are shared. Brands like Gucci, Timberland and Nisolo are promoting ethical production of leather and transparency in their supply chains to promote the longevity and durability of leather products and guarantee the provenance of their products.

Simone leather shopper by Nisolo

Cotton

Cotton is a natural fabric produced from cotton seeds which grow to form long fibrous strands of raw cotton. These strands are then picked, and the fibre is spun into yarn.

Cotton material can be made from traditionally grown chemically treated cotton, sustainably produced organic cotton or recycled cotton. Cotton is produced in different ways and traditionally has a high water footprint, but innovations in production have reduced water consumption in the finishing process of cotton by 96 per cent. Cotton yarn can be woven to different thicknesses and into different types of cloth, such as canvas and denim. The material can be finished in a range of colours and coated to make it waterproof or more durable.

The density of a cotton fabric will affect the weight of a bag. For example, a bag made of canvas, which is a denser material, will be heavier than one made of cord. Cotton is usually coated with wax, using a technique originally used in ship sails in the nineteenth century. Waxed materials have a glazed finish and are used extensively to create fashion accessories, providing an alternative to leather hides. The materials are durable, waterproof and similar to leather in that they acquire an aged appearance over time. Cotton fabrics are biodegradable, and recycled cotton fibres are often combined with other fabrics to add strength.

Cotton canvas is a staple material for most brands. Spanish luxury brand Loewe introduced their Balloon shoulder bag as a new signature piece crafted from canvas combined with a leather trim. Canvas has also been used by Celine, Louis Vuitton, Prada, Barbour and many more.

Polyurethane (PU)

The main material, other than leather, used in fashion bags is a type of plastic called polyurethane or PU; also called 'synthetic leather', PU is used extensively in footwear, fashion bags and accessories as a cheaper and vegan alternative to

Opposite: Loewe canvas and leather Balloon bag

Right: Annex Vegan backpack in PU from Matt & Nat's Loom collection

animal leather. It has also been used as a replacement for PVC (polyvinyl chloride), which is the most environmentally damaging plastic of all.

PU can be made out of recycled plastic bottles, and both virgin and recycled PU can be made to look and feel indistinguishable from genuine leather. PU can be manufactured in a range of colours, textures and finishes that emulate all the variations of leather hides but at a much lower price. Because PU does not have the restrictions of leather skins in terms of size and imperfections, it is cost effective and less wasteful during manufacture. It is ideal for mid- to lower-priced bags but has been used throughout the industry at every level.

The downside of PU is that the material is not breathable and does not 'wear in' like leather. It can be torn and cannot be easily repaired, so PU bags are quickly discarded once they are damaged. While fewer resources are used to make PU than other synthetic materials, like all plastics it is originally made from fossil fuels and does not decompose. Designers such as Stella McCartney, Comme des Garçon and Matt & Nat have all used PU to create fashion bags and accessories.

Left: Nylon striped weekender bag by Longchamp
Opposite: Adwoa Aboah with nylon Prada bum bag

Nylon

Nylon is a synthetic plastic derived from crude oil. It can be processed into yarn and was originally developed in 1935 as a substitute for silk fabrics. Nylon has gone in and out of fashion for clothing but has been a favourite for fashion bags and accessories at every level of the market since Prada re-imagined nylon as a luxury fashion bag fabric in the 1980s and 1990s. Nylon has the advantage of being lightweight, durable, strong, foldable, easily dyed and water-resistant, properties which make it a perfect fabric choice for bags. Lightweight nylon weekend and travel bags made out of woven nylon fabrics like ripstop have revolutionized the

luggage market due to their weight, excellent flexibility and ability to expand and regain shape. Nylon has also been used for more functional casual bags, such as festival and sports bags, and to create backpacks, bum bags and totes, for both Prada and Longchamp.

Like other synthetic fibres, nylon is not biodegradable. However, recycled nylon, often made from nylon fishing nets, can be produced using fewer resources than original nylon. Brands such as Prada are supporting initiatives to incorporate recycled nylon into their product ranges.

Polyester

Polyester is a synthetic thermoplastic, meaning it can be melted and reformed. Although it was invented in 1941, polyester became popular in the 1970s when it was used in brightly coloured materials for casual clothing and disco wear. This gave polyester a reputation as a cheap fabric. Polyester is commonly used for making bags that are foldable and lightweight. The material takes printing inks well and is ideal for creating branded printed bags and backpacks used extensively as reusable promotional giveaways.

As polyester bags are made from plastic, they do not break down and biodegrade easily. The sheer amount of plastic waste produced each year has encouraged innovative solutions to recycling polyester by melting down existing plastic bottles and re-spinning them into new polyester fibre. There is no difference between recycled polyester and virgin polyester in terms of performance, durability or strength. Brands such as SKFK have pioneered the use of recycled polyester fabrics in their bag ranges.

Acrylic

Acrylic is a strong transparent plastic material made in sheets which can be bonded together and moulded using heat. The first acrylic bags were created out of a trademarked material called Lucite, invented in 1931 by DuPont. Lucite is a durable acrylic material originally intended for military use during World War II. After the war, the trend for modern materials saw acrylic plastic material like Lucite and Perspex® (Plexiglas®) adopted for use in fashion accessories. Acrylic materials can be shaped, dyed, textured, produced in any colour or left clear, and made to imitate tortoiseshell and ivory. Acrylic is tough and durable but can be easily scratched. The manufacturing process can release toxic fumes and the material is not biodegradable, although it can be reused.

The popularity of acrylic plastics has not diminished, and they remain extensively used for fashion bags, particularly clutch styles. Cult Gaia, a Los Angeles-based brand, created one of fashion's most famous IT bags using acrylic plastic. Its half-circle contemporary Ark bag is constructed of jointed acrylic pieces woven together.

SKFK recycled nylon and polyester tote bag

Cult Gaia acrylic half-circle Ark bag

Neoprene

Neoprene is a synthetic rubber produced from the chemical chloroprene. It was first developed in 1930 and was initially used for a range of different products such as tyres, wetsuits and hoses because of its strength and water-resistant properties. As well as being a practical material, neoprene has been used to make high-end clothing and accessories. Neoprene has a soft, padded texture and is formed from two layers of fabric bonded together. It can be cut without its edges being sewn and comes in different thicknesses, making it flexible but still able to hold its shape.

Japanese Bag in neoprene by MM6 Maison Margiela

Choosing the Right Materials

Selecting the right materials for bags takes research to build knowledge of different materials and their individual qualities, and experience to know how to apply materials that will enhance rather than detract from a design. As new materials are developed all the time, materials research is ongoing.

Many materials are not easily available and have to be ordered at trade shows, such as Première Vision and Lineapelle, or directly from tanneries, manufacturers or merchants. A visit to a trade show is a good way to amass a lot of knowledge in one place and develop connections with suppliers. Trade shows are usually biannual, working at least six months in advance of a selling season, and provide a useful overview of global trends in materials and colours and highlight new material developments.

Increasingly, sustainable and ethical materials for bags that avoid environmental, social and economic harm are forming part of mainstream trade shows. There are also shows, like the Future Fabrics Expo, that specifically showcase globally sourced sustainable and ethical materials, including leather alternatives. These commercially available materials have a low environmental impact. Designers such as Paguro, Matt & Nat, Stella McCartney, Vivienne Westwood and BOTTLETOP have used their creative vision and knowledge to repurpose materials or source sustainable alternatives, working with small producers, manufacturers and communities. This has broadened the concept of commercial production to include **fair trade** initiatives that help producers in developing economies achieve sustainable and equitable trade relationships.

Functions of the Material

The majority of good quality fashion bags are made in leather using full-grain calfskin because of its quality and natural appearance. **Full-grain leather** refers to the strongest and most durable part of the hide of an animal, which is just below the hair. It preserves the imperfections or marks found on a natural skin and has not been buffed to remove them. A bag is, however, rarely made of just one type of leather or material. There are a whole host of materials that are part of the body of a bag or are used in the interior but not seen. The different types of materials used to make a bag need to be considered and have a high degree of compatibility. This can be more important in relation to the unseen elements within a bag.

The natural characteristics of a material are a primary consideration relative to the design and aesthetic of a bag. Denim and leather, for example, are strong and durable materials with a character-istic ageing that makes both improve over time. A denim bag with leather handles or leather trims may convey a workwear aesthetic and both fabrics are strong and durable. A lightweight nylon bag using woven tape for straps or fastenings may be synonymous with sportswear or a casual weekend bag, but both materials are lightweight and strong and can be both decorative and functional.

Vivienne Westwood Ethical Fashion Africa collection, S/S 2012

Leather zip-top bag with contents

The design brief also directs material choices through price, function, styles in a range, market level and particular issues a brand may focus on like fair trade principles, recycling or sustainability. If a range includes soft bags and small leather goods, different leathers and reinforcements will be required. Soft and unstructured bags require different materials to bags with more defined silhouettes.

Bags get heavier the more they carry so it is important to consider the function of a bag in relation to the weight of its materials, including reinforcements, linings and hardware, which will all add weight and thickness. Identifying stress points on a bag, or areas that may need to be protected such as corners and handle attachments, or the base to stop damage when a bag is put down or picked up, should also be considered if more than one material will be used for the body of a bag.

Reinforcements

The 'unseen heroes' of bags, **reinforcements** exist between the outer body that shows off the design and aesthetic of a bag, and the lining that hides the interior structure. They perform a functional role to increase the performance and life of a product.

They can be as important to the look of a finished bag as the outer body materials used and should be selected with care. Using the wrong reinforcements can destroy the natural characteristics of a material. Reinforcements can stabilize stretchy leather skins, making materials easier to cut and stitch, or add strength to areas on the bag where handles, fittings, zips or components are attached to the body. They also support the base of a bag so it does not collapse when empty or distort when full.

Reinforcements come in as many varieties as materials, so testing their fitness for purpose is essential to make sure they can do the job required of them. They come in woven and non-woven forms and can be glued onto leather or fabric, or are pre-printed with glue to be attached using heat. There are also many different thicknesses. Thicker reinforcements make the materials more robust and able to hold structure and very fine ones can provide just enough support to retain a look of lightness. The properties of reinforcements always need to match closely to the design, aesthetic and core characteristics of a material so no element of a bag functions in opposition to its natural properties.

Weekender combining canvas and leather

Other types of reinforcement used in bags include card and fibre boards that can add stiffness to structured shapes and are used to produce a more structured look or to make suitcase-like constructions. Aquiline, a synthetic plastic, is the most commonly used material inside bags to create structure. Foam can be used to give a soft padded look, ideal for quilting techniques, or add volume without adding weight to soften shapes and increase body.

Linings

The linings of fashion bags serve to hide the interior structure of a bag; they need to be long lasting and of a sufficient quality to match the other materials used. One of the most common issues with bags is that linings wear out before the bag does.

Linings should be seen as more than a functional element to a bag. They present a design opportunity to provide a visual boost when a bag or accessory is opened, particularly if printed in bright colours or made from a combination of different materials. Linings often carry the branding and include details such as pockets, interior zips, divisions, different coloured edge bindings and piping.

Combining Materials

The key points to remember when selecting materials are that the characteristics of all the materials used in a bag must be similar and related to its style, aesthetic and function.

Whether designing for a brand or for yourself, the selling price of the bag will dictate the sorts of materials that can be used and the consumer's expectations of a product in terms of design aesthetic, quality of materials and manufacture. The most expensive bags are usually made in the most expensive materials. Many brands have signature materials that they like to use each season to meet a level of quality and excellence in craftsmanship expected by consumers.

In addition to these factors, it is now essential to consider **design for disassembly** when selecting materials. A product must be designed so that it can be quickly, easily and cost-effectively taken apart at the end of its life and the components reused, recycled or **upcycled** (reusing materials to create a product of higher quality than the original). The right combinations of materials in any one product can make it more or less sustainable.

99

Why Leather?

Leather is an animal hide that is cleaned and treated using a process known as tanning to preserve its natural qualities. Leather's attributes include strength, flexibility, breathability, friction resistance and the potential to be water- or heat-resistant. It can be both soft and supple, and mouldable and firm, making it the ideal material to use in a bag where different parts behave in different ways and require different properties. The handles of a bag, for example, need to be strong and keep their shape, while the body of a bag may be softer. Leather is perfect for making bag components such as straps, attachments and more decorative items like tassels and lacing.

Tanning

The benefits of utilizing dried animal hides were first recognized in prehistoric times. The earliest recorded leather artefacts date back to 1300 BC and techniques to soften and preserve hides were used by the Ancient Greeks, Egyptians and Romans, who used leather to make protective clothing and armour. As the use of leather grew, so did the scale of manufacturing and the tanning processes used to create it. Tanners and leather craftsmen formed trade guilds during the Middle Ages in order to maintain control of the quality and supply of leather using traditional vegetable tanning.

Vegetable tanning is a skilled process that takes up to two months and is mainly done by hand. The process uses vegetable tannins rather than mineral or synthetic tanning agents. It starts with the preparation of skins, which are de-haired, degreased and desalted. These are then soaked in water and put into vats filled with natural tannins,

like tree bark, before being dyed and sealed with wax to create rich, deep-coloured hides. Veg tanned leather develops a patina, a sheen on the surface through wear as it ages, which has helped put the 'luxury' into leather.

In 1858, the Industrial Revolution brought about a new, quicker and cheaper process of tanning using chemicals. This alternative method to veg tanning was called **chrome tanning**, a process that used chromium salts to streamline the manufacturing process. Chrome tanning eliminated many of the preparatory steps required for traditional veg tanning.

Both veg tanned and chrome tanned leathers are used in the fashion industry today. Veg tanned leather has a reputation as a premium product due to its quality and painstaking labour-intensive production. The leather lasts for generations and, as hides are initially stiff, they have to be worn in and improve with age. Veg tanned leather holds its shape and is produced in natural earthy colours that darken with age, making it ideal for heritage and menswear brands. It can be used in raw-edged bags, where edges are polished and stained to give a hand-crafted quality finish, and suits techniques like moulding and embossing.

Chrome tanned leather is quick and cheap and does not require as much skill to produce; colours and finishes of chrome tanning know no bounds. Leathers are produced in bright, intense colours which remain unchanged during the product's lifespan, and in a multitude of finishes in response to the constant innovation expected in the fashion industry. Hides are thinner and softer than veg tanned leather but not as durable.

Both veg and chrome tanning have an environmental impact. The process of chrome tanning is particularly harmful as it creates toxic wastewater that can have serious consequences for animal and human life if left untreated and allowed to enter the water system. However, such is the global demand for varied, cheaply produced leather that today 90 per cent of all leather produced worldwide is chrome tanned.

Types of Leather

Leather is sold as individual hides or bundles of whole skins of animals and priced by the square foot. Each hide or skin is unique to a particular animal and includes blemishes and marks, so no two leather hides or skins are ever the same.

There are several different types and qualities of animal hides and skins so it is important to know the characteristics and sizes of each, although they can all be produced using veg or chrome tanning.

Hides are from the largest animals like cows and range from 12 square feet to 35 square feet. They are sold as whole or 'full' hides. **Sides** are hides that

have been cut down the backbone of the animal into two half pieces.

Skins are from smaller animals, such as sheep and goats, and usually range from 4 square feet to 9 square feet. Sheep skins can be produced as skins with wool on the outside, which are soft, stretchy and porous and mostly used for clothing or for trims on bags and gloves, or as full-grain leather. Skins are often tanned using a special chemical process to produce **nappa leather**. Nappa leather retains the beauty of the original hide but is extremely soft and flexible and does not crease. Sheep nappa leather is used for high-end luxury products and was originally used by Bottega Veneta to develop its signature Intrecciato weave to make its nappa leather strong enough for bags.

Goat skins are used to produce high-quality full-grain leather that is fine and soft and usually used for gloves, shoes and bags. After falling out of fashion, goat leather has enjoyed a revival. Billy Tannery is a small pioneering tannery producing sustainable, bark tanned goat leather made in England, which they manufacture into a range of luxury goat leather accessories.

Kips are the skins of younger animals that are not fully grown, so smaller in size than adult hides and skins. Other hides, such as snake, alligator, crocodile, lizard, kangaroo, ostrich, deer and fish, are used on a smaller scale, mostly at the luxury end of the market. The spectrum of exotic leather can be much larger, comprising some endangered species, due to increasing demand for rare exotics skins. Many major fashion houses, including Prada, Chanel, Hugo Boss, Victoria Beckham and Mulberry, have now stopped using exotic skins.

As well as different sizes of skins, leather comes in different grades that indicate the number of times a skin has been sliced or 'split' and the quality of its grain. **Splitting** is a process where the skin is cut into

Billy Tannery rust grained leather
hand-held bag

different layers of thicknesses that deteriorate in quality as more splits are made. **Grain** refers to the density of fibres in each layer of the hide or skin. The top split, which is closest to the outer skin of an animal, has the densest fibres and is used to make full-grain leather noted for its strength, durability and quality. Considered the best leather for leather goods and fashion bags, it is the only leather that can be aniline dyed. Aniline dyeing means dye pigment goes through the hide or skin giving a translucent sheen and does not just sit on the surface of the leather.

The more splits to hides and skins, the lower the grade of leather because they are taken from the lower, thinner layers, making them less durable than full-grain leather. Top split full-grain leather has not been sanded or buffed to disguise imperfections, but lower grade splits have surfaces that are reworked to resemble a higher grade of leather.

They can be given textured finishes like **suede**, where the flesh side of a hide or skin is buffed creating a soft raised pile or 'nap', or **nubuck**, which is a similar process that buffs the grain surface of leather.

Embossed leather mimics exotic skins such as crocodile, lizard and snake. After embossing, where a design is stamped on the surface, leathers can become stiff, but this technique works well on areas of a bag or for small leather goods. **Two-tone leather** has two layers of pigments applied; the top colour is uneven and shows the contrasting colour underneath to create an aged look. **Patent leather** has either a liquid resin coating or a layer of plastic laminated onto the top layer of leather to produce a shiny surface. This reduces the stretch in the skin, making it suitable for belts and some bag styles. Many of these finishes are used in fashion bags where designers sometimes like to use a certain type of leather to build an identity for a band or particular collection.

Leather Alternatives

The fashion industry is one of the most polluting industries, but it is a vital one for global economic growth. In its desire to create a more sustainable, greener fashion system, and in response to an explosive growth in consumer trends toward recycled, vegan, eco-friendly and fair trade products, many fashion accessories brands have begun to explore sustainable and ethical materials as commercial alternatives to leather. The natural alternatives being trialled for use in accessories include cork and bark fibre reinforced with polymers, and innovative leather substitutes derived from pineapple, coconuts, grapes, coffee, mushrooms and seaweed. Many are emerging as viable alternatives to leather along with repurposed and upcycled materials.

Ocean Plastic

There are estimated to be 51 trillion pieces of plastic in our oceans. A single plastic bag can take 20 years to decompose, plastic bottles last as long as 450 years and fishing line 600 years. The frightening escalation of plastic pollution in the oceans has created an opportunity to develop a new non-natural material that is being used within the fashion industry. Parley for the Oceans is an environmental global network that aims to collaborate with brands and designers to explore environmental initiatives. Working with adidas they have created Parley Ocean Plastic™, a material created from marine plastic waste. This recovered raw material has been used by adidas to make trainers and sportswear. Parley have created their Ocean Bag range of totes, working in collaboration with several contemporary artists to create a series of limited-edition bags.

Parley for the Oceans x Doug Aitken tote bag made of reclaimed Ocean Plastic™

Reina rubber shoulder bag by Paguro

Rubber

Every year millions of rubber tubes are sent to landfill, so there are clear environmental benefits to reclaiming rubber. Synthetic rubber is not biodegradable so this glut of tyres and innertubes presents a huge resource perfect for re-imagining into innovative products that go beyond the soles of shoes. The textured matte finish of rubber and its strength make it a perfect choice for fashion-forward bags. Brands such as Paguro have reinvented recycled rubber to create innovative fashion bags that are a real alternative to leather. Paguro also use a wide range of other reclaimed and repurposed materials, including reclaimed canvas.

Microfibre

Lorica® and Vegetan® are two branded non-woven synthetic fabrics that match the characteristics of leather. They are lightweight, washable, breathable and have similar lifespans to leather. Originally developed for Japanese fishermen, Lorica® is made from **microfibres** (fine fibres produced from a blend of tightly woven polyester and nylon) soaked in resin, which results in a supple, durable material. It comes in a range of colours and can be printed, cut, stitched and bonded, making it a viable substitute for leather when making accessories. It has been used by Kaanas to make their Lantern bag. Vegetan® is a microfibre material specifically designed as a leather alternative, with less environmental impact than some vegan leather options as it is more biodegradable.

Cork Leather

Cork leather is made from the bark of cork oak trees, making it a natural alternative to leather. It has a unique finish and is waterproof, stain-resistant and durable, qualities which make it an excellent choice for accessories. Although making cork leather is a lengthy process, bark can be harvested multiple times and trees have an average lifespan of around 200 years. The cork is sliced into thin sheets and attached to a reinforcement to strengthen it. The unique appearance of cork leather has already appealed to several luxury brands, including Chanel and Bottega Veneta, who have used cork in their accessory ranges.

Chanel cork shoulder bag

Wood Leather

NUO, originally developed as Ligneah, is one of the best-known fabrics created out of wood and is a soft, flexible material with a leather-like texture. NUO is already established as a material used in the fashion industry for bags and smaller accessories.

Wood used to make NUO is ethically sourced and treated to make it more supple and soft. Its surface can be given a smooth leather finish or embossed finishes such as crocodile and python effects. NUO Design (formerly OOD) produced a line of accessories to showcase the fabric, which is dedicated to slow fashion and innovative solutions to sustainable materials.

Flexible Stone

Flexible stone is a new product made from layers of rock that have been extremely thinly sliced and mounted onto a cellulose fleece reinforcement giving strength and flexibility. This natural material has a variance in its colour and texture like leather, so no two pieces are the same. The stone becomes flexible enough to act in a similar way to traditional leather and is already being used for computer cases, bags and belts. It is also being used for fashion accessories by pioneering Berlin-based bag brand Luckynelly to create its luxury fashion bags.

Green and yellow wood textile
hand-held bag

Piñatex silver shoulder bag by Taikka

Mushroom Leather

Mushroom leather is an environmentally-friendly organic material developed from mushroom spores and plant fibres. This lightweight leather alternative is created using the waste material from commercial oyster mushroom production. After harvesting the mushrooms, the remaining material is shaped and dried and mixed with hemp and linen fibres. It can be dyed, has a suede-like texture and is completely biodegradable. It is extremely lightweight and flexible too, which makes it effective in a wide range of products. Mushroom leather has been used by designer Stella McCartney for her iconic Falabella bag, which was exhibited at the Victoria and Albert Museum's exhibition 'Fashioned from Nature' in 2018.

Mushroom leather Falabella bag with silver chain handle

Piñatex®

Piñatex® is made from cellulose extracted from the leaves of the pineapple plant, a by-product of the agricultural fruit industry. A natural leather substitute, Piñatex® leather has become a viable commercial alternative to leather and is well established within the fashion industry. The fabric is strong, breathable, supple, lightweight, flexible and easily cut, stitched and printed. It comes in various thicknesses and finishes, making it perfect for footwear, fashion bags and accessories. Piñatex® has been widely used across the fashion industry by brands such as Hugo Boss and H&M and fashion labels like Taikka.

Cactus Leather

The Mexican-founded brand Desserto has
pioneered cactus leather production and introduced
it to the fashion industry. Cactus leather is made
from harvesting mature cactus leaves, which are
then dried and softened and made into a durable
alternative to leather using a patented formula.
Unlike other vegan leather alternatives, the process
does not use plastic derivatives. This gives Desserto
the potential to make the vegan leather industry far
more sustainable and has the advantage of using
very little water in production. Already producing a
range of accessories, Desserto have collaborated
with other fashion brands.

Banana Leather

Pineapple fibres used to make Piñatex® are not
the only fruit fibres being used to create leather
alternatives. Bananatex® is a durable, waterproof
leather substitute made purely from banana plants,
which are self-sufficient and require no chemical
treatments. Strong fibres are stripped from the
banana plants for processing and the leather-like
fabric suitable for accessories is produced. This
organic material is made in the Philippines in
collaboration with Swiss bag label QWSTION, who
design a range of bags using this innovative fabric
that effectively utilizes natural resources.

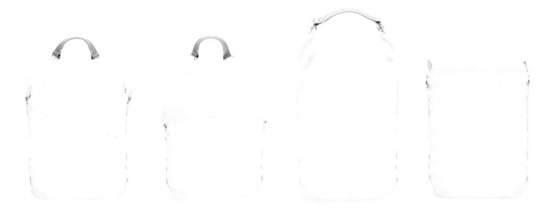

Banana leather backpacks and
large hobo bags by QWSTION

MAGNETHIK corn leather tote bag

Orange Leather

Italian textile company Orange Fiber is making textiles using waste orange fruit fibre after the production of orange juice. The company uses an innovative technology to weave the cellulose fibres into sustainable fabrics. They are working with Salvatore Ferragamo, the luxury leather goods company, on a capsule collection to service the growing demand for high-quality sustainable materials and products in the luxury fashion sector.

Apple Leather

Alongside orange leather, apple leather is a popular alternative to leather that is currently being used in the fashion industry. Apple leather also uses waste from juice production, which is hydrated, ground and spread onto a canvas where it moulds into a fabric similar to leather. Apple leather is long lasting, strong and ultra-violet (UV) resistant, and has been used for fashion bags and accessories by brands and designers, including Alexandra K and Happy Genie – who have produced commercial ranges using the material.

Corn Leather

Corn is one of the most widely grown cereals in the world. Once the ears are harvested, the remaining waste plant material can be ground into powder and then mixed with resin and wood pulp which supports the resin layer. This semi-natural leather substitute is a strong, durable and versatile material with a feel very similar to animal leather. Sustainable French footwear brand Veja have created the Campo range of vegan trainers using corn leather, and accessories designers Alexandra K and MAGNETHIK use corn leather in their collections of bags and accessories.

Kombucha Leather

A symbiotic colony of bacteria and yeast, or SCOBY, is the natural film that grows on the top of kombucha teas. This cellulose film does not require chemicals in order to be produced and is considerably cheaper to make than other types of leather substitutes. SCOBY leather is versatile, can grow in any shape, be dyed and is 100 per cent biodegradable. It has the advantage that it does not need to be sewn together, as pieces can stick together and dry as one. Initially the material has the feeling of parchment, with a translucent appearance. Although not widely used in the fashion industry yet, several companies, including Malai and ScobyTec, are developing kombucha leather for the mainstream market.

Paper Leather

Paper leather, made from recycled paper blended with cotton fibres, as well as from tree bark and leaves, has been used in the fashion industry to make bags, backpacks and accessories for several years. These bags are strong, water-resistant and biodegradable, making paper leather a viable alternative to animal leather. Prominent in the luxury bag field, Bottega Veneta made its woven clutch bag using washi paper derived from the bark of the Japanese kōzo (paper mulberry) plant. This sophisticated raw-edged bag featured the brand's signature weaving technique, a silk lining and stylish blackened hardware, and set a new benchmark in sustainable products.

Designers like Ilvy Jacobs are also using paper leather to create tactile, directional fashion bags with sustainability credentials.

Tree Bark Leather

Made from sustainable fast-growing timber, tree bark leather is similar to cork leather. Each piece is individual because of its natural wood grains and is strong, durable and flexible enough to be sewn. It can be cut into very thin layers and used for garment making, bags and footwear. Brands such as ATLR RSVD have used tree bark leather to design their ranges of crossbody bags. Dolce & Gabbana has also used this material in its fashion bags and footwear ranges.

Left: Bottega Veneta paper leather handbag, A/W 2012–13

Opposite: Dolce & Gabbana tree bark bag, A/W 2013–14

Malai

Malai is a leather alternative made using waste coconut water sourced through the coconut industry in India. It is produced using a similar process to kombucha leather. The coconut water waste produces bacterial cellulose refined to form sheets of the Malai material, which can then be dried and dyed. The material has a touch similar to both paper and leather and is being used to create a range of interior products, bags and accessories.

Grape Leather

VEGEA is an award-winning sustainable fabric production company who use a toxin-free and solvent-free method to create leather from wine waste. Produced from grape peels, stalks and seeds, this 100 per cent vegan leather transforms fibres and vegetable oils present in grapes into a material with all the characteristics of animal leather. It uses zero water and zero oil in the production process so has no negative impact on the environment. Grape leather comes in the natural tones of wine, such as

blush, Bordeaux and burgundy, and can be printed to look like animal skins such as ostrich and snake. The leather can also be produced on a commercial scale. Brands such as H&M use it to make vegan bags and shoes in collaboration with VEGEA. French brand Maison Peaux Neuves uses this grape leather from Italy for all its range.

Ultrasuede® BX

In 1970, Japanese textile maker Toray created a synthetic material called Ultrasuede®, which has been used in interior design, cars and the fashion industries. In response to a need for greener, more environmentally-friendly synthetic materials that utilize waste resources, Toray have now created the world's first suede-like non-woven fabric using plant-based raw materials. Unlike the original Ultrasuede® fabric, Ultrasuede® BX is made of 30 per cent plant-based materials. It also contains polyester derived from waste sugarcane and polyurethane made from waste castor oil. This gives the suede-textured material a soft feeling and durability. It also makes it stain resistant.

Maison Peaux Neuves grape leather
Haut les Coeurs shoulder bag

113

5
Product
Development

The most exciting moment for any designer is seeing a design drawing come to life as a three-dimensional object. In order to make this possible the steps from design to product realization follow a series of stages to test, refine and resolve products.

A successful designer understands the **product development** process to bring a product from a concept to a finished, marketable item, and over a period of time builds the skills and experience necessary to know how to easily realize a drawing into a three-dimensional object. With practice the problems of constructing a bag can be resolved at the drawing stage, but initially it is easy to draw a design that a product developer might struggle to make. The art of successful product realization revolves around familiarity with the manufacturing process, enabling a designer to realize a design without having to compromise a concept. The importance of product development can never be underestimated; a good designer with the knowledge to translate a two-dimensional drawing of a design idea into a three-dimensional, fully-resolved product becomes a more effective designer in light of this knowledge.

Transforming a Drawing into a Bag

There are craft skills associated with accessory construction that have been developed over generations, but manufacturing methods do not stand still and contemporary processes like 3D imaging, printing and laser cutting have been integrated into modern sampling and manufacturing processes. Although designers are not responsible for every technical aspect, they have to be familiar with the way in which things are produced by artisanal craftsmen or mass produced in factories where processes are staged and repeated multiple times.

As with the design stage and materials selection, designers need to research how things are made, which should be ongoing. Even if they are working with the support of a technical team, the more knowledge of the product development process the better. This may mean unearthing traditional craft techniques and reappraising them for a contemporary audience. Archives, specialist collections or vintage pieces are ways to start this form of product development research in order to understand the process of making. Many brands have archives, including some like the Ferragamo Museum in Florence, Italy, which are open to the public. Research will most certainly involve investigating contemporary and future developments and considering how these will impact on current practice. It may involve deconstructing objects to understand how volume is created from a flat pattern, examining the reinforcements used inside a bag and seeing how these vary, and studying the hardware used or the position of logos and the techniques used to apply them. It can be valuable to look at areas outside accessories to see if there are techniques or new processes applicable for fashion bags and accessories.

So what are the stages of product development? The process for product development will vary from bag to bag and style to style but the basic steps can be summarized as the following.

1. Finished design
2. Source outer body materials
3. Source components, fabric linings and reinforcements
4. Decide on embellishments
5. Draft a pattern
6. Create a first sample (prototype) to test the design concept and product development process
7. Refine through a process of adjustments and full or partial mock-ups
8. Make a final resolved production sample

During the design development stage, 3D sampling using small quarter-scale or half-scale mock-ups are useful tools to problem solve areas of a bag and take a fraction of the time to construct compared with full-scale mock-ups (see pages 84–5 and 125).

Once the final range of bags has been decided, a **signature piece** (a piece that reflects the personality and values of a brand) is usually selected to be made as a first sample or prototype and should represent the product that is the most technically difficult to make. Ranges are connected by construction techniques, materials, details and colour, so a bag that uses techniques and details incorporated widely across the rest of the range solves the most problems and provides the greatest knowledge to be used across the range.

Preparation

Accessories are formed into three-dimensional shapes from a two-dimensional pattern that is cut based on the technical drawing, so the clarity of information in a technical drawing or tech pack is vital for accurate patterns to be cut.

The design of a bag can be complicated and, unlike a shoe which is built over an existing foot shape or 'last', a bag is not usually built over an internal structure unless it is a moulded or a vacuum-formed (where a sheet of plastic is heated and stretched over a shape to make a mould) product. The structure of a bag has to come from the pattern shapes stitched together to create volume. The choice of materials and seams will support or soften the bag structure. Through **gussets** (pieces of material sewn into a bag to enlarge parts of it), folds or pleats, volume can be created, essentially so a bag can function as a container. Even flat accessories like wallets have small gussets, folds or pockets used to accommodate the items carried within them.

Before pattern making and construction begins materials need to be chosen, as they will affect the way in which a flat pattern is constructed and the width of seam allowances required to enable pieces to be stitched together. Hardware also needs to be considered at this stage, not only for its functionality but also because it is the 'bag jewellery' that

enhances the aesthetic of a product and bears the name of the brand. Hardware can make as much of a statement as the silhouette or colour of a bag so should never be considered as an afterthought. As it adds weight and thickness, and needs to be attached to a bag, patterns must allow for this. Custom hardware should be sampled well in advance. Independent or smaller designer studios may not, however, be able to commission custom hardware as it can be costly and time-consuming to produce. If off-the-shelf hardware, which is made in standard sizes, is used, it should be sourced before patterns are cut. It can be plated into different colours and finishes, which can have a dramatic effect on the overall look of a product, or combined with a custom component, significantly reducing costs. In terms of cutting patterns for straps, fastenings or flaps it is essential to know the hardware being used before starting.

Suede bag shoulder bag with decorative hardware detail on the straps and front

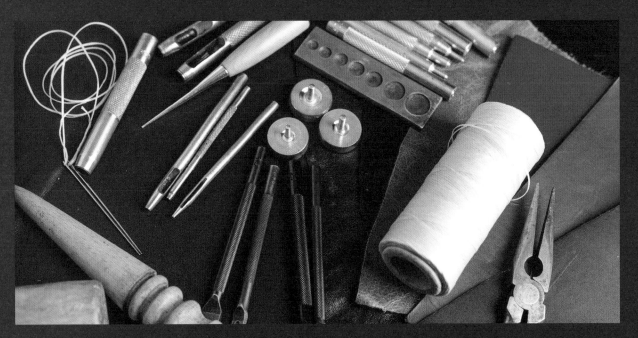

Tools and equipment for making leather accessories

EQUIPMENT BASICS

Working in leather or leather-like materials requires a well-ventilated workshop or studio space and specialist tools and sewing machines which can stitch into hard-to-access areas of an accessory. Listed below are the basic hand tools needed for pattern cutting.

Awl: A sharp spike used to pierce holes in leather or material before stitching.

Bevelling tool: Used to soften the cut edges of belts and straps to give a finished look.

Bone folder: Used to crease or fold down seams once they have been stitched.

Clicking knife: A cutting knife used to cut freehand and also for **hand skiving** (thinning down the thicknesses of leather).

Cutting mat: Used to protect work surfaces, cutting mats come in various sizes and materials.

Dividers: Two adjustable metal arms used to add seam allowance (extra width) to pattern pieces so they can be stitched together.

End punch: Used to neaten and shape the tips and ends of leather belts and straps.

Hand skiving tool: Used to reduce thickness and bulk of leather hide/skin.

Leather scissors: Scissors with one serrated blade to prevent leather and leather-like materials from slipping when cut.

Mallet: A type of hammer with a head made from wood or nylon used for flattening seams.

Pliers: A hand tool for holding objects.

Pricking iron: Used to create holes in leather for hand stitching.

Revolving punch: A punch with different sizes of hole used for strap details, rivets and eyelet setting.

Single punch: A conventional hand punch with just a single sized hole for functional or decorative uses.

Steel hammer: A useful tool when attaching buckles and rivets.

Steel ruler: A metal ruler used to cut patterns in paper and pieces of leather.

Strap cutter: A hand-held device with a blade inside used to accurately cut long strips of leather belts for bag straps.

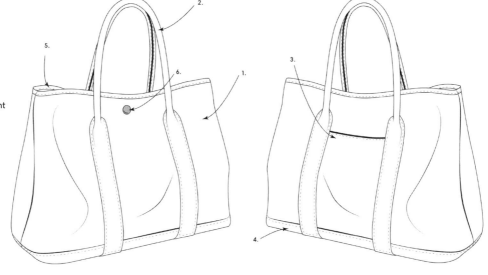

1. Body

2. Strap

3. Side pocket

4. Bottom reinforcement

5. Binding

6. Stud fastening

Anatomy of a tote bag

Pattern Drafting

At the design stage a significant amount of experimentation to mock-up areas of the bag that may be problematic or need more resolution has already taken place, along with basic testing of potential materials to see how they respond to heat, glues, machine or hand stitching and skiving. Even a simple bag can include several component parts that differ from style to style, so it is a useful exercise for designers to familiarize themselves with the key pattern pieces in a bag. The diagram above shows the pattern pieces for a tote bag.

Pattern drafting (drawing the template pattern pieces that are individually cut and sewn together to make a bag) is a central part of the process of creating a product. It will determine the proportions of the bag, its construction and types of seams and details used, as each will affect the way in which a pattern is cut. A pattern is the first step in conveying

information to a technical team about how to create a three-dimensional prototype from flat pieces of paper or card. Initially, the proportions of a bag must be decided. A quick method to establish these is to draft the front of the body of a bag to scale on a piece of card, drawing on elements such as pockets or flaps, and hold the template against the body. This will give an opportunity to decide whether proportions should be scaled up or scaled down. Bags usually come in standard dimensions and a brief may require specific sizes to meet function or cost constraints. More experimental proportions and scale are associated with innovation and more directional designers. By making a bag bigger or smaller it looks more original and will stand out from competitors' products. Adjusting proportion also allows for a successful style to be scaled up or down within a range, so a make-up bag can be scaled up to create a tote bag or handbag style.

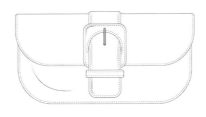

Design drawing showing different proportions of a bag shape

119

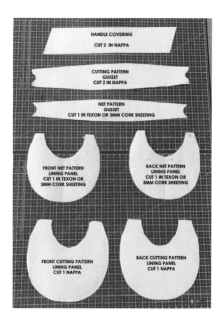

Flat pattern pieces of a bag by Serena Bashir

Patterns need to be made using accurate measurements, with seam allowances added for assembly. The pattern must then be checked to make sure that pattern pieces fit perfectly together before it is cut out in materials for samples or mass production. In preparation for sampling, it is useful to make a simple full-scale mock-up in card or paper at this point to test the pattern and decide on the positioning of components and the width of straps and fastenings.

First Sample

The first sampling stage conveys to members of the design team and product developers the physical reality of a design or range of bags and ensures everybody understands the way the finished product range should look. The first sample of a prototype indicates the potential of a finished bag, which may then be developed into further colour variations, different materials or different proportions. If all previous stages have been completed effectively, a first sample should look similar to the technical drawings in a tech pack, but still leave room for fine-tuning of the design and experimentation.

Even with years of experience it is difficult to get a bag perfect within the first sample and inevitably there will be changes to the proportions, detailing or construction lines, or changes to improve function, ergonomics or to reduce costs.

The sampling process is expensive and to reduce costs initial samples can be made in calico, felt (which can be thinned, moulded or left as a raw edge, like leather), or Salpa, a leather substitute commonly used in industry for prototyping.

As the samples are refined, they are made in the same materials as those intended for production, including reinforcements and linings, so that any changes are relevant to the final product. The constraints of a material always need to be understood and must be suitable for the type of bag made and behave predictably during manufacture. More importantly, the combination of materials needs to be compatible, and the materials need to have similar lifespans. In terms of disassembly, the sampling process should address the following questions: What happens to a bag at the end of its lifetime? How easy is it to separate materials out to be recycled or reused?

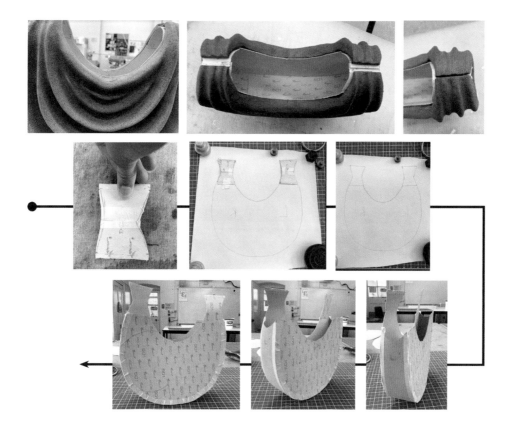

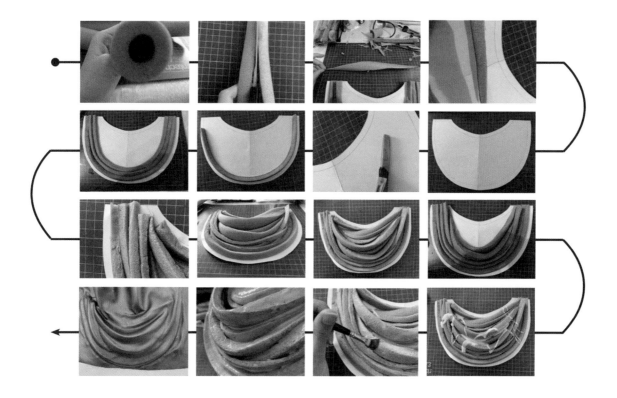

Images of mock-ups showing the development of outer body of a bag by Serena Bashir

Construction Considerations

It is important in product development to consider the construction of a bag, including the style of edging and seams to be used, the type of construction (one-piece, two-piece or multiple-piece), and the order of assembly.

Edging and seams

Accessories use several different kinds of edge and seam finishes, all with their own characteristics. There are three main types – raw, turned and butted – all of which can make a difference to the final appearance of a bag. The finishes can be used individually or combined so different constructions are used in one product. This will be determined by style, function, materials, cost and ease of manufacture.

Raw edges are cut, unfinished edges stitched on the outside of a bag. They suit thicker veg tanned leathers and can be used as a prominent design feature. Raw edges can be polished, a popular technique used on heritage pieces. Raw edges can also be sealed to prolong the life of a product, or dyed in dark or contrast colours more suited to high-end fashion bags. Many leather substitutes do not give a clean-cut edge and cannot be used in raw-edged products. Clean-cut edge construction also eliminates bulk and thickness, so areas where seams meet and form a bulky join need to be refined at the pattern stage even though leather can be thinned or skived down, a process of slicing layers of leather away to produce thinner areas which can be joined together more easily.

Turned edges are stitched in a similar way to garments, where all the stitching of seams is on the inside. Turned edges make neat and refined final products and are widely used across a range of different leathers and leather substitutes. An edge is thinned or skived, and then glued and folded over. It can be top stitched or left plain.

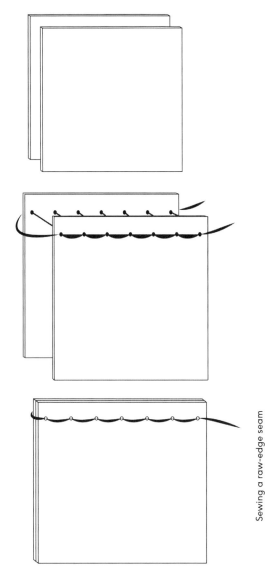

Sewing a raw-edge seam

Turned seams, where two raw edges are stitched together and then glued or stitched flat, are suitable for softer leathers and suedes. Stiffer veg tanned, heavily embossed or patent leather cannot be turned once stitched, so cannot be used in bags that have turned seams.

Butted edges have no seam allowance and are laid next to each other to meet edge-to-edge without an overlap. They can then be stitched together. This type of edge is used for hand-stitched items or very stiff leathers. **Butted seams** are turned and glued and then both layers are stitched. This type of construction is often used on specific areas of a bag, such as gussets.

One-, two- and multiple-piece construction

In its simplest form, a bag can be made from two pieces of material stitched together like a pencil case. This is known as **two-piece construction**. It has a small volume, so a limited capacity to contain things.

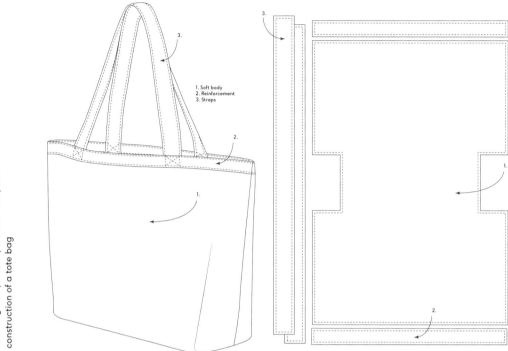

Tote bag and pattern piece for one-piece construction of a tote bag

1. Soft body
2. Reinforcement
3. Straps

One-piece construction is a way to build in volume through the inclusion of a base. When stitched together a triangular-shaped base is formed at the bottom of the bag with enough volume built in to enable the bag to expand once used and 'sit' on a flat surface. The most common one-piece construction is the T-base bag, where a stepped shape is cut into the pattern. When sewn together this forms a T shape at the base of the bag. This basic construction has been widely used in everything from make-up bags to iconic totes and is the starting point for more difficult constructions. The ability of a bag to sit is important for point of sale, where bags are placed on shelves.

With more complex constructions, the body of a bag can be made up of multiple pieces to form the sides. These can then be stitched to a base. A flap to fasten the bag, pockets, handles and straps can all then be positioned and added. The key point to remember is that a bag has an inward facing side

carried against the body and an outward facing side away from the body. Similarly, it has a top, a bottom and ends. Pockets, fastenings, straps, handles and hardware all have to be positioned with this in mind to make the bag functional, ergonomic and attractive.

Assembly

Once a full pattern is drafted, the order of assembly should be considered. Before an accessory is stitched together the sequence of attaching each element needs to be worked out. This is not always as obvious as it may sound, for example a zip closure may need to be stitched in first before sides are joined. What is possible in sample production is not always the same as in mass production, with its very separate manufacturing operations. The mocking-up process and first sample will clarify the order of assembly and which elements need to be attached at the relevant points.

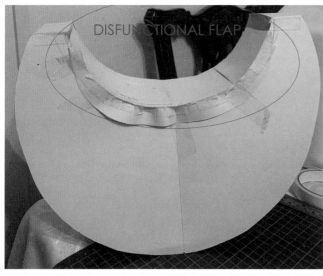

Correction to a mock-up and (below) first sample of the finished bag by Serena Bashir

Final Sample

Once a first sample is produced it is a designer's responsibility to carefully assess any changes that need to be made. Approaches for doing this are to place masking tape over areas and draw on corrections, or print out photographs of relevant views of a bag and draw directly onto these. This is the stage where everything needs to be finalized and further experimentation cannot take place. To communicate effectively with manufacturers, product development teams will want clear instructions from a designer about changes affecting the aesthetic, function or ergonomics of a bag.

The final sample should be a result of all these corrections and as close as possible to a finished bag. The type of company or brand the bag is being created for will determine if the sample is made in-house or by an external manufacturer. It is usual practice to make a final factory sample, which is signed off as the definitive production sample against which mass production will be assessed in terms of quality, function and cost.

Sustainable Manufacture

Every year the fashion industry uses billions of litres of water for production, resulting in polluted wastewater. It ships millions of products around the world, contributing to global carbon emissions, and huge quantities of waste textile and plastic fibres are either incinerated, sent to landfill or end up in our oceans. It is clear the fashion industry cannot continue to utilize resources in such an unsustainable way and overconsumption of fashion products cannot continue to grow. The fashion industry's fast fashion model aggravates the problem through its fast-paced design and manufacture cycles of low-cost items. It is not a question of if this cycle should be slowed down, but when the industry will reinvent itself as a more sustainable circular system.

The fashion industry is the world's third-largest manufacturing sector, so the task to reinvent the industry and become more environmentally friendly will focus on how products are designed, produced, sold and reused. Where products are made and the conditions under which they are manufactured are becoming increasingly important to consumers. Changing the mindset of consumers to be aware of the environmental impact of their purchasing choices is also necessary, and designers will play an essential role in sustainable design practice that feeds into the manufacturing cycle. Building new technologies into design, product development, manufacture, longevity and the supply chain is key to creating a sustainable circular fashion system.

The following questions should be asked if a bag is made from leather:

- What are the ethical practices in raising animals to use for hides and tanning into leather?
- Does the brand use sustainably sourced materials or recycled fabrics?
- How is the product made and who makes it?
- Are workers across the supply chain paid fair trade wages and working in safe conditions?
- Does the brand think about its environmental footprint? Does it work to reduce waste, energy use and carbon emissions?
- Does the brand contribute to communities through charitable donations or supporting community initiatives?
- What happens post-consumer to a product at the end of its lifetime and how can it be disassembled and reused?

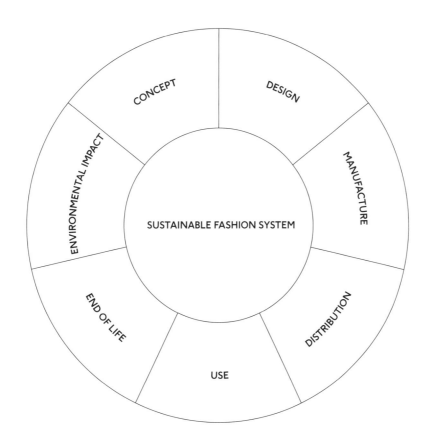

CONCEPT

DESIGN

MANUFACTURE

ENVIRONMENTAL IMPACT

SUSTAINABLE FASHION SYSTEM

END OF LIFE

DISTRIBUTION

USE

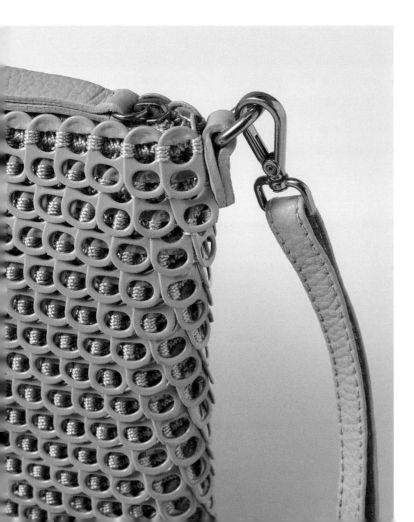

Left: The Luciana recycled bottletop bag by BOTTLETOP

Above: Mylo™ mushroom leather by Bolt Threads

Edge sealing and polishing in the Hermès workshop

Longevity

Many brands have expertise in manufacturing certain leathers and have mastered particular constructions and techniques to an exceptionally high level of craftsmanship. These will feature in their collections over a period of years, creating signature design styles and constructions which make products that last for years.

Most notable of these brands is Hermès, founded in 1837 to make harnesses. Hermès is renowned for its craftsmanship and exacting standards of excellence in every aspect of manufacture. The brand employs several thousand leather craftsmen in its ateliers and each craftsman spends two years learning the handcraft leather techniques that the brand has been using for over a hundred years. Each artisan is

supervised by a master craftsman during this period to make sure everything they produce is perfect. It takes one artisan between 15 and 24 hours to make a bag using a classic saddle stitch, a signature of a Hermès bag. Saddle stitching involves a long piece of waxed linen thread with a needle attached at both ends. The needles are passed through holes pre-punched into leather pieces to be stitched together. By passing each needle through the holes one continuous running stitch is formed. Saddle stitching requires consistent movements to achieve a straight line of stitching, which, unlike machine stitching, does not produce stress points on the thread, making it strong and durable; even if the saddle stitch breaks, it will not unravel.

After the leather is cut, each artisan is responsible for making a particular bag from start to finish and once completed the inside strap is stamped with the number of the workshop, the year of manufacture and the individual craftsman's serial number. If the bag is damaged in use, a customer can send it to the same craftsman for repair.

Artisans learn, and are expected to master, all the specific techniques needed to construct Hermès core designs, such as the Kelly bag. The brand's manufacturing techniques are used extensively across all its other bags, so this core design is essential to master. All bags are entirely hand stitched and hand skived. Each of the individual elements are saddle stitched together using two needles to give perfect uniformity and finish. Stitches are flattened with a hammer, making them smooth to the touch, and the raw edges of bags are polished with sandpaper and a hot ironing tool to remove any excess glue and to attain an even edge. Afterwards the leather is coated in

beeswax to seal and protect it from humidity and give it a tactile, smooth finish.

The Hermès production capacity is very limited, and quantities are kept low in order not to compromise quality. Even the amount of gold used in the bag locks, clasps and feet has not been reduced so that fittings on contemporary bags have the same patina as the older ones. The brand's most famous and costly bag, the Birkin bag, takes each artisan 48 hours of work to create. All iconic Hermès bags, such as the Kelly and the Constance, are also meticulously manufactured. A Hermès bag is created through traditional craft techniques and exceptional skills to have the longevity to last several lifetimes.

The diagram below shows the elements that make up a Hermès Birkin bag, and where handcrafted techniques are applied.

Anatomy of Hermès Birkin bag

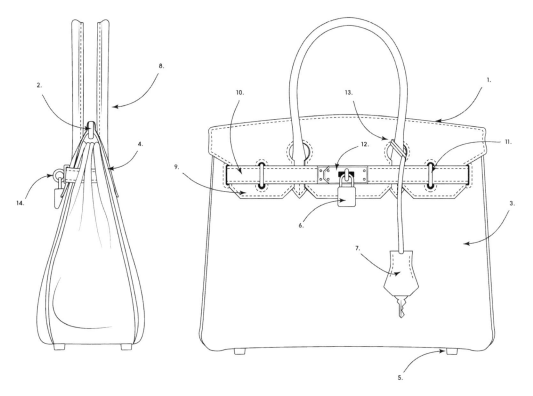

1. Hand saddle stitching
2. Polished edge
3. Polished bees-waxed body
4. Turned edges
5. Gold feet
6. Gold lock
7. Clochette
8. Top handle
9. Flap detail
10. Sangles
11. Pontet
12. Plaque
13. Tiret
14. Touret

Innovations Through Technology

It is clear, when it comes to design and product development, that there are a number of initiatives which can be put in place to produce bags and accessories in more sustainable and ethical ways. The obvious choices start with ongoing materials research and an awareness of the exciting innovations. The tanning of leather has serious environmental implications. Several innovations around greener tanning have already been developed for commercial use. ECCO Leather, one of the world's largest tanners, has taken a lead in a sustainable solution to leather production. Its trademarked DriTan™ leather is a groundbreaking tanning process that uses the moisture already present in leather hides. The resulting leather is indistinguishable from traditionally tanned leather in terms of its quality, characteristics, stability and in production time. Not only does the process save enormous amounts of water, it also significantly reduces the potentially harmful wastewater produced during conventional tanning.

A large part of the environmentally damaging process of accessory manufacture is caused by the use of glues. When used to stick reinforcements onto leather these can make it impossible to separate elements of a bag at the end of its life, making recycling impossible. As traditional solvent-based adhesives are so damaging to the environment and harmful to health, a new generation of less polluting, water-based adhesives have been developed for industrial use. These new greener adhesives offer a low risk to human health and the environment and have been developed to be used in smaller quantities. They are also non-flammable and do not give off the strong smells associated with conventional solvent adhesives.

A host of new materials are being developed that take advantage of natural waste products from the food and agricultural industries, such as coffee grounds, fruit, wood and paper pulp (see pages 105–13). Existing synthetic materials, such as rubber and plastic, are also being reused, recycled and reinvented (see pages 103–4).

Designers and brands across all levels of the fashion industry are also addressing the issue of waste, particularly the amount of waste material produced when pattern pieces are cut. The idea of **zero waste** ensures the tools to reduce, reuse and recycle are embedded in design practice and product development. In terms of resources, once all the pattern pieces of a bag are cut out, a significant percentage of material is wasted in the gaps between each pattern piece. Small adjustments to patterns can minimize this, saving a considerable amount of material. The individual nature of each leather hide or skin means that up to 50 per cent of a cowhide can be wasted because of scars and blemishes. However, some sustainable practices have traditionally existed in bags and accessories, as hand-cut pattern pieces can be positioned so the smaller offcuts and waste pieces in between can be used to make small leather goods.

When designing an accessory, a designer and product developer also need to carefully consider how to design and make a product in a way that it is easy to disassemble. For design for disassembly to become common practice, it must be embedded at the initial design stage. The way a bag is designed affects its ability to be dismantled and reused.

Simple decisions about fabric combinations have significant impacts on design for disassembly. Using material reinforcement and linings that are made from several different fibres makes recycling more difficult. For example, an easily removable 100 per cent cotton lining in a bag is easier to reuse than one made of a synthetic blended fabric.

At the pattern stage, the larger each pattern piece is, the easier it will be to reuse. Using fewer pieces

Gretel 3D printed bag by XYZ

reduces the time it takes to disassemble a bag and will make the initial production costs cheaper because fewer pieces are cut and stitched together. Different components in a bag, such as metal fittings like clasps, locks, eyelets, studs and zips, may all be made out of different materials and hard to sort once disassembled. Care labels that accurately list materials facilitate disassembly and recycling.

Three-dimensional product visualization systems have the potential to make the greatest impact on design, product development and manufacture by eliminating the laborious, expensive and wasteful process of creating first prototype samples.

Three-dimensional printing of components is well established and, as commercially offered printing services have become increasingly sophisticated and accessible, 3D printing using a range of materials – including plastic, metal, porcelain and rubber – is now easily accessible. In what is considered a 'zero waste' printing process (because only the exact amount

of material needed to print each component is used), all waste can be avoided. It also offers the ability to customize products easily and cheaply. The ability to customize and create one-off products cost effectively has been the driving force behind the uptake of digital manufacture. Three-dimensional manufacture has been embraced by Austrian precision craftsman Published By and Italian bag brand XYZBAG, who combine traditional and digital craftsmanship to produce unique fashion bags. Its bags form an extensively customized range printed using nylon powder.

The role of technology in building a more sustainable fashion system is evident in almost every area, from smarter, greener materials to less wasteful manufacture, from the tracking of products throughout their life cycles to monitoring sales in order to manufacture less. Technology has paved the way for a new breed of digital designers whose aim is to design in a virtual environment.

6
Technology and Design

The fashion industry has been slower than other industries to capitalize on the advantages digital tools can offer. It has cocooned itself in an environment where tactile physical objects still predominate and, since the early 2000s, the industry has subscribed to a model of fast fashion where high fashion designs are rapidly mass-produced at low cost leading to overconsumption. Increasing scrutiny of current practice has spotlighted ethical and sustainable issues and the waste, high cost and time associated with designing, sampling and manufacturing physical ranges. Some brands are turning to digital solutions to create a new industry model that embraces a growing trend for 'immaterial fashion', embedding digitization at every level of the creative and product development process.

New digital toolboxes offer designers the opportunity to test creative boundaries, to make samples cheaply and accurately, streamline manufacturing processes and embed sustainable practice. This enables brands to be responsive to consumer needs while curbing overconsumption. Consumers can engage with fashion brands in a different way through different digital interfaces. The new digital toolbox appeals to a generation of designers who are digital natives and have been steeped in technology for most of their lives.

The Digital Fashion Designer

The digital fashion designer aims to create and test the properties of designs in a virtual environment.

Through the use of digital materials libraries and digital tools – such as body scanning and 3D pattern manipulation, visualization, rendering, prototyping and printing systems, as well as augmented reality (AR) and virtual reality (VR) – digital designers can create fashion bags and accessories that are indistinguishable from physical objects. The digital fashion designer can also co-create, customize and personalize new types of bespoke one-off accessories manufactured at a fraction of the cost of handmade items.

A digital fashion designer requires the same creative flair, global cultural knowledge and awareness of trends as any designer, but the creative environment they may find themselves in is different to that of a conventional design studio. A digital fashion designer is just as likely to be working alongside someone from the gaming or film industry, or a technology expert, as a traditional pattern cutter or sample maker, because the digital design world encompasses elements of innovation from many other disciplines and industries. The digital design studio is a collaborative environment where designers explore and execute evermore inspirational and innovative ways to create products digitally and connect consumers with a brand through digital platforms. The digital fashion designer is fluent in all the main CAD software used for sketching and visualization and has an eye for rich imagery, drifting seamlessly from one digital interface to another. They also have an eye on new technological developments across an array of disciplines and the vision to consider how these can be adapted to fashion design and product development.

American designer Tommy Hilfiger (b. 1951) has been one of the first to recognize the importance of digital design and has incorporated 3D design technology into all his design teams to enable a fully digital design process from first idea to finished product. The brand has developed a set of digital tools, including digital patterns, colour and materials libraries, digital 3D presentation tools and rendering technology, which has transformed all design and sample production stages into virtual processes. His collections are then shown through the brand's 3D digital showroom. This has eliminated elements of the design process, such as physical drawing and sample making, speeding up the sampling process by 50 per cent. Nothing is manufactured except for catwalk pieces and products to sell in shops, which minimizes time, resources and costs. In collaboration with Stitch Academy, a technology incubator dedicated to embedding 3D thinking in the fashion industry, Tommy Hilfiger has developed a talent pipeline of digital designers, pattern cutters and visualizers who will work across all product categories.

The most significant development and groundbreaking use of 3D imaging has come from Hanifa, the Congolese fashion brand designed by Anifa Mvuemba (b. 1991). Hanifa collections have debuted on social media using 3D virtual clothing without models. As yet Hanifa's collection of accessories only includes jewellery and shoes, but it is only a matter of time before bags are also featured.

Smart Technology in Fashion Bags and Accessories

The connection between creative design and digital technology is not new and fashion bags have always been the focus of attention for technologists as a way to individualize products or improve function and reflect changing lifestyles. The main focus has been on the smartphone and its connection to bags – amalgamating fashion and a phone-charging function. One of the first and most successful of these bags is Ralph Lauren's Ricky Bag, a traditionally crafted leather bag that can charge a smartphone and has an internal light operated by an inside flap. This subtle application of technology paved the way for more accessories with smart functions.

Emmy Rossum with Kate Spade Everpurse handbag

Innovative Fashion Bags

Fashion bag brand Kate Spade has had a long collaboration with Everpurse to develop a series of fashion-forward leather bags, consisting of two tote bags and a wristlet (a small bag that attaches around the wrist with a thin strap). The items have built-in smart pockets to charge iPhones using lightweight wireless technology.

As technology has advanced, design ambitions have increased to consider a much closer bond between science and design to improve not only the function of bags but their aesthetic too. Innovative designers are now required to co-create or collaborate with a range of specialists to make products that may have several functions, many of which are linked to our smartphones and portable tech.

For the environmentally conscious, Diffus Design created a solar-powered bag that has integrated

Louis Vuitton OLED digital screen bag

solar cells to charge a mobile phone or laptop. Rather than taking the standard approach of placing solar panels onto the outside of a bag, Diffus Design collaborated with an embroidery specialist and the tech savvy Alexandra Institute in Denmark to find a more innovative yet still functional solution which did not compromise the bag's contemporary aesthetic. The surface of the bag is embroidered with a combination of normal embroidery and conductive embroidery which conveys the energy collected from the hundred solar sequins (small solar-powered units) to the powerful lithium battery hidden in a small compartment. During the day, the solar units generate enough electricity to charge a mobile device and the

battery. Opening the bag in the dark activates optical fibres attached to the inside of the bag, providing a soft diffused light to find items by.

The Unseen, a London-based collective, has pioneered the connection between science and design through its colour shifting leather bags, which change colour based on user interaction or changing environments. Each bag responds individually to its user, offering unique customization and individuality. The brand's range features a calfskin backpack that responds to air pressure changes, which affect the surface colour of its leather. The range also features an alligator-skin shoulder bag with environmentally responsive ink

which changes to reflect the different seasons, turning black in winter, red in spring, blue in summer and green fading to red in autumn. Other items in the range change colour based on body temperature, touch, wind and sunlight.

The fusion of advanced technology and design led luxury brand Louis Vuitton to launch versions of its iconic monogrammed fashion bags with built-in flexible Organic Light-emitting Diode (OLED) digital screens. These functioning screens utilize technology originally developed for use in smartphones to allow a fashion bag and phone to become one.

Eclipse smart bag by Diffus Design

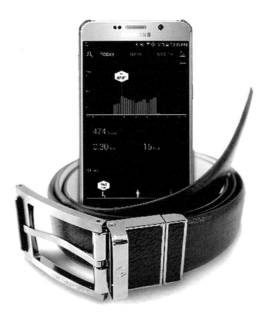

WELT smart belt

The bags show moving images on the revolutionary OLED screens incorporated into the sides. These screens are the thinnest, highest quality ever made. This blending of digital imaging technology with the brand's signature pieces represents a breakthrough that moves wearable tech away from novelty light-up bags or built-in simple charging functions, to a fashion bag with a real connection between the aesthetic and technology used within it.

Wearable Accessory Tech

Wearable technology is not confined to smart bags. Small leather goods and other accessories like belts have been a source of inspiration for designers, scientists and technologists. A leather belt is usually seen as purely functional, but belts are now being used to blur the lines between medicine, technology and fashion. Communications giant Samsung launched the WELT belt, a belt with an advanced internal structure to monitor activities while being worn. This smart belt monitors physical health and activity during the day, measuring waist size, eating habits, movement and inactivity. It combines this information and processes it in an app that recommends ways for the user to improve health and be more active.

The importance of the WELT belt in the digital design landscape is that it is a fashion item developed by a communications company.

Augmented and Virtual Reality

It is not just communications companies that are advancing into traditional fashion areas, however, but also game developers. Much of the technology developed for gaming is utilized in 3D visualization software used in the fashion industry for digital design and product development, but this is not a one-way relationship. Brands have capitalized on the popularity of computer games to reach young audiences by offering gamers virtual high-fashion clothing and accessories as a means of virtual self-expression.

Louis Vuitton designed virtual accessories with its signature monogram pattern in collaboration with Riot Games for their League of Legends game. The virtual and physical worlds merged when League of Legends' virtual collection inspired a physical collection of clothes, bags and shoes. Meanwhile, digital fashion houses such as The Fabricant, creating digital-only clothing for our digital identities, have emerged.

Technological advancements are not limited to design and sample creation but increasingly in how products are sold to consumers. **Augmented reality** (an interactive experience of a real-world environment) and **virtual reality** (a simulated experience similar or different to one from the real world) are being applied in creative ways in the fashion industry to address the 'try before you buy' philosophy engrained in consumers and to show features of products realistically. This has been made easier by apps that enable virtual try-ons and 3D animations that allow consumers to see products from different angles, essential for bags and shoes. These technologies are revolutionizing the way consumers buy and shop. UK brand Burberry has been at the forefront of integrating technology into the shopping experience, continuously

Hemdrok Jacket by The Fabricant in collaboration with Zeeuws Museum. A 3D reimagining of an 18th-century garment as contemporary clubwear.

experimenting with digital innovation. In collaboration with Google, Burberry has launched a new augmented reality smartphone shopping tool that gives an accurate idea of what the product looks like before it is purchased. The product can be searched for using Google and an accurately scaled image is shown against other physical objects. French luxury brand Dior is also using augmented reality to enable consumers to try on sunglasses using their smartphones.

This technology is not confined to luxury brands but is being developed across the industry. Sportswear brand Puma and online retailer ASOS are developing apps that offer consumers a new way of viewing products using virtual reality.

Puma augmented reality app, Wanna Kicks

New Tech Accessories

Accessories are often gateway products into brands and attention is now firmly on tech accessories as the fastest growing category. Portable tech, once seen as a necessity, has become an exciting new area of design and materials innovation where technology, science and design meet. These new tech accessories are particularly important to luxury brands who generate large profits from accessories. While the accessories may be small and less imposing than a statement bag, they have hefty price tags attached, and brands are increasingly including them in their ranges.

Phone Case

Smartphones have become widely accessible so it is hardly surprising they now form a large part of the tech accessories category. The phone case sits within the protective small accessory genre and essentially emerged as a practical way to protect phones. They are made in a range of materials, from carbon fibre, leather, wood and plastic to precious metals.

Each model of phone needs a specific case, usually made of a single layer with moulded edges into which a phone can be positioned. Holes are cut in the back and sides so that the features of the phone, like the camera, volume buttons and on/off switch, can still be used. Alternatively, the case can be a slim sheath into which the phone is slipped.

Since they first emerged, phone cases have skyrocketed in price and currently form part of every accessory range. Award-winning brand Mous has led the way. Its signature wooden smartphone cases are a simple but stylish cover that slips over the

Smythson leather phone case

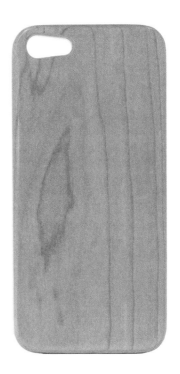

phone but can then be joined to other accessories through a modular system. At the designer end of the market, brands like Hadoro, Celine and Loewe have produced leather alternatives that are bespoke, stylish or fun offerings.

Earbuds and Headphones

Ever since the advent of the Sony Walkman in the 1970s, portable music has given rise to a range of accessories, and the advent of wireless technology has facilitated the earbud. The small size of earbuds makes them more portable than headphones and they can be easily slipped into a bag, pocket or

stylish carrycase. Must-have items include the Louis Vuitton Horizon Earphones. These wireless and Bluetooth enabled earbuds were made in collaboration with premium audio tech company Master & Dynamic. They come as a monogrammed pair of buds in a leather charging case.

Quality luggage manufacturer RIMOWA are known for their aluminium suitcases. Their future-facing collaboration with electronics giants Bang & Olufsen created the H9i limited edition headphones, contained in a signature RIMOWA aluminium case. The headphones are made in leather and the same aluminium material as the luggage.

RIMOWA/Bang & Olufsen headphones
and carry case

Smartwatch

Watches and watch cases have been given a state-of-the-art upgrade to take their place in the new order of smart tech accessories. A collaboration that brought together Apple technology and the craft heritage of Hermès resulted in the Apple Watch Hermès collection. The watch face has a colour-changing display that reflects its leather strap. The buckle references the equestrian heritage of Hermès and is attached to interchangeable straps.

Charger

Portable tech needs constant charging and, just like other items with their origins in functional roots, the charger has entered the list of tech accessories. For example, Berluti, which has a rich history of making luxury leather goods, has turned its attention to tech accessories by producing a fine-crafted leather covered charger. Meanwhile, tech brands such as

Kreafunk are also creating chargers that bridge the gap with fashion.

144

Smythson leather laptop case

Laptop and iPad Cases

The more constructed padded and protective leather laptop cases may be large enough to be considered as small bags, but generally they are either flat folders that zip up to secure a laptop or sleeves into which a laptop or tablet can be slipped. The difference is largely functional and depends on day-to-day use, for example travel requirements or a need for extra protection.

Laptop cases come in every fabric imaginable and across a wide price range. Dutch brand CoverBee designed an $11 million laptop sleeve covered in over 8,000 diamonds and a black sable fur trim. More modestly priced but still luxury laptop cases are included in ranges by Tom Ford, Prada and Mulberry.

CoverBee diamond encrusted laptop case trimmed with sable fur

145

7
Other
Accessories

Small leather goods are items carried around in bags or pockets to hold objects such as coins, credit cards, keys and make-up. They also have a protective function, for example eyewear (glasses and sunglasses), earbuds, headphones and charger cases, laptop and tablet holders, and travel items such as passport holders, bum bags, luggage tags and watch cases. Hybrid products like bag charms can also be classed as small leather goods. As a product category, small leather goods have changed since the early 2000s to reflect our more mobile and technology-driven lifestyles. Cheque book holders have largely disappeared with the advent of payment chips and cashless transactions, and as make-up compacts are now manufactured out of cheaper materials, gone too are leather compact holders.

When designing a range, designers put together a family of products unified through details, materials or construction. It is easy to imagine that smaller pieces are given less consideration. In fact it is more challenging from a design perspective to integrate smaller items into a range to give them the same design handwriting as larger signature pieces. Materials may be different too; often small leather goods are made in leather, but they could equally well be made in materials such as nylon and other synthetic textiles.

Flat Accessories

The flat family of small leather goods are united by the fact they are made with very little volume and largely do not need much ability to expand to hold contents. They can be challenging to integrate into collections of bags because of their lack of volume and do not have as much allure as other items in a range due to their functional nature.

Card Holder

Slightly bigger than the various cards it holds, a card holder is a single function product. The rectangular holder is made as a series of flat pockets stitched together. The pockets are large enough for the cards to be slipped in and out of but still fit snugly.

Leather card holder

Wallet

Wallets are generally constructed as larger versions of the card holder to house credit cards, bank notes and coins, and some personal items. A wallet has multiple pockets and small gussets to accommodate bulkier items like coins, and generally folds in half to be secured with a fastening or has a zip fastening along the top edge. Wallets were once thought of as men's accessories, but now appear in both men's and women's ranges with slight styling differences.

Orange leather wallet with multiple pockets

Passport Holder

The passport holder is a simple folder that opens out like a book, into which a passport fits. They sometimes have credit card pockets but usually only have one function.

Passport holder

Key Holder

Key holders are usually flat folded pieces of leather or material secured by a fastening. They unfold to reveal clips onto which keys can be attached. Key holders have been eclipsed for the most part by the sportier key fob, usually a long piece of folded leather or cut leather that can be attached to a key chain or key ring.

Luggage Label

Leather luggage labels belong to a past era of travel, but stylistically they have refused to disappear from small leather goods ranges. They provide a branding opportunity or a chance to offer customized photo images or monogrammed pieces. They are usually two pieces of leather stitched together with a buckle and strap to attach them to a bag.

Above: Aspinal of London folded leather key holder

Right: Prada leather bag with luggage label

Three-dimensional Accessories

Small leather goods ranges can also include a number of three-dimensional accessories, such as purses, make-up bags and eyewear cases. They are used by more expensive brands to create accessible and affordable branded pieces offered to a wider range of customers without losing any of the cache or exclusivity of a luxury brand.

Decorative butterfly bag charm by Aspinal of London

Sabina leather coin purse with silver frame by Maxwell Scott

Bag Charm

Bag charms sit between traditional small leather goods and tech accessories. Although rarely smart, with little built-in technology, they are decorative and highly noticeable items which have emerged as one of the most popular new accessories. Bag charms are designed specifically to be worn on a bag and are an amalgamation of jewellery, key rings and luggage tags. They are made in multiple materials, precious stones, leather and metal, and have become collectable items and an important source of branding. South Korean bag brand MCM has built one of the largest ranges of collectable bag charms across its collections of backpacks and bags in its signature logo-printed material Cognac Visetos. Hermès, Coach, Louis Vuitton and many other brands also include the bag charm.

Coin Purse and Purse

Still very much present in small leather goods ranges, the coin purse is an item that may have outlived its functional value but not its aesthetic one. A coin purse is usually a miniature simple T-base construction, or gathered into a frame, to provide enough space for small items, essentially no bigger than coins, which need to be carried around. The difference between a purse and coin purse is size; the purse being a larger version. Functionally, however, the purse has fallen out of fashion in favour of the wallet, which allows for more internal organization of credit cards, money and personal items.

Make-up Bag

The next size up from the purse is the make-up bag, usually bearing the name of its brand, and, for practical reasons, rarely made in leather. Make-up bags tend to have a T-base construction and a zipped top, and be lined with a waterproof or washable fabric.

Eyewear Case

The three most common accessories are shoes, bags and eyewear. Eyewear now comes in every possible style and eyewear cases have been upgraded from a geeky necessity to a confident fashion statement, coming in a wide range of styles and construction.

Body Conscious Accessories

A wristlet was once a small bag with a thin carry loop attached that dangled sedately from the wrist. In keeping with more active lifestyles it has migrated up the arm to become an armlet, and is often associated with sports and fitness. It can include the technology to carry and charge a phone while exercising. This use is reflected in the styling and fabric choices and armlets are often made in neoprene, a form of synthetic rubber, or nylon.

Bum Bag or Fanny Pack

A bum bag or fanny pack is a waist bag that evolved from money belts into a small leather good. Usually a fabric pouch worn around the waist or hip like a belt and secured by an adjustable strap, this functional bag had a reputation for being perfect for hands-free travel in the 1980s. The popularity of streetwear and the emergence of athleisure has seen the bum bag become an important item from luxury brand collections to fast fashion ranges.

T-base white make-up bag

Tiffany & Co eyewear case and glasses

Sports armlet with smartphone holder

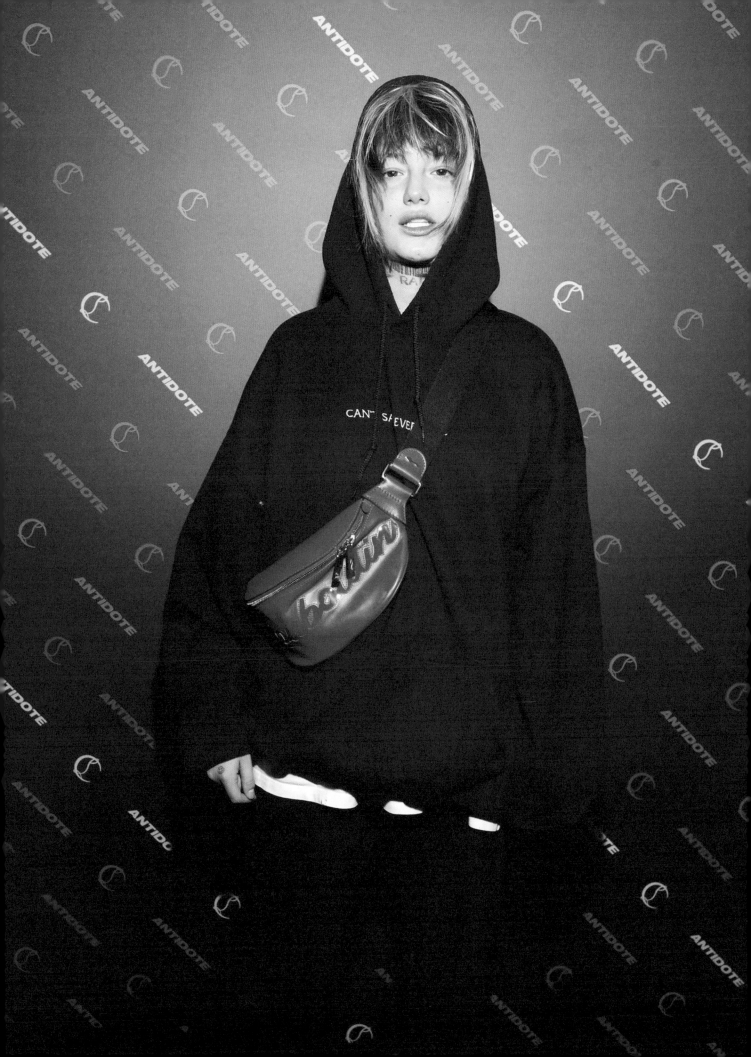

Footwear

The most exciting thing about being a shoe designer is the starting point, the human foot. Unlike bags, shoes are built around a structure and are made to take its shape. The first decision a shoe designer makes is to 'redesign' the human foot by selecting the shape of the foot-shaped mould or 'last' they want to work on, around which the final shoe will be formed. A last can be a natural shape, or directional and innovative, like Alexander McQueen's Armadillo shoes – an eerie reinvention of the human foot.

A **last** can be used to create a particular type of footwear such as a trainer or a sandal. With the exception of soft slippers, all shoes need to be made on a last. The last represents a foot in its most natural or stylized form. The closer to the natural shape of the human foot, the more comfortable a shoe will be as it replicates the true characteristics of a foot. However, fashion trends reflect the reinvention of the human foot to define different eras, which are reflected in the toe and heel shapes of shoes. For example, the stiletto heels of the 1960s, the platform shoes of the 1970s or the futuristic trainers of the 2000s. Shoes reflect clothing styles and tend to follow the same trend cycles, with higher heels worn when certain styles are on trend and lower heels with others. Think of the slim silhouettes of the 1920s and the elegant Louis heels that accompanied them, or the shoulder pads and chunky heels of the 1940s. There are more women's footwear styles than men's, but for both men and women there are numerous functional styles, like waterproof or protective footwear, and dozens of fashion styles.

Alexander McQueen Armadillo shoe

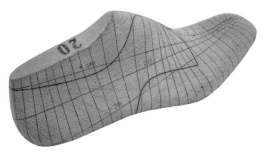

Wooden last

Chlobocop wearing Louboutin bum bag

The role of a shoe designer is part creative fashion designer and part engineer, as a shoe carries the weight of the body. A shoe designer needs to understand the characteristics of a foot – that they are asymmetrical with uneven soles and insteps – as well as the walking action of the foot and how a shoe affects this, and how a shoe stays on the foot or how it is taken off. Shoes need to fit perfectly and a few millimetres extra in a footwear pattern will make the difference between a shoe that is comfortable or one that is ill-fitting. Shoes can be delicately handcrafted to the highest standards using traditional techniques or mass-produced in factories using specialist machinery.

Much like accessories, there are hidden parts of a shoe that provide it with its shape, support and function, for example the thick cushioning mid and outer soles of trainers. Shoes use reinforcements and have stiffeners added at the toe and heel so that once the shoe has been built around the last and is removed, the shoe retains its shape.

Lasts are made in different sizes and heights and for each shoe size and heel height a new pair of lasts (left and right feet) are required to make a pair of shoes. Lasts need a set of components, such as **heels**, **stiffeners**, **insole boards** and soles, that match each last. Initially, all the lasts and components needed create significant development costs in the sampling and manufacturing processes so designers should consider the balance between creative design and production costs when designing a commercial range of shoes.

Once the toe shape and height of heel are decided (flat, mid-height or a high heel), the lasts, components and materials should be chosen.

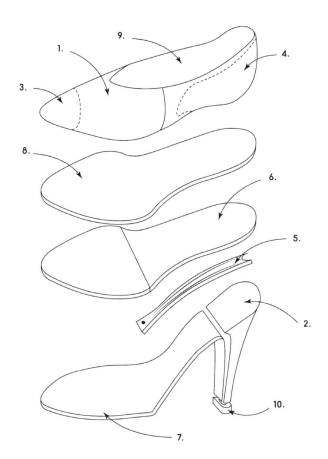

Anatomy of a shoe

1. Upper – top part of a shoe

2. Heel – attached to the bottom of a shoe, elevating the shoe to different heights

3. Toe puff – support for the toe shape of a shoe

4. Heel stiffener – support for the back heel area of a shoe

5. Shank – a metal stiffener used on high-heeled shoes to retain the pitch of the last

6. Insole board – a template of the button of the last onto which the upper part is joined

7. Sole – the underside of the shoe that touches the ground

8. Sock – used to hide the internal structure of the bottom of the shoe and provide cushioning

9. Lining – used to hide components like stiffeners and the internal structure of the shoe

The breathable, mouldable and durable nature of leather makes it the perfect material for shoes. Shoes can also be made out of synthetic materials and fabric, but these do not have the same longevity or breathability as leather shoes and the materials have to be mouldable round the curved toe and heel areas.

The design stage follows the process common to the fashion industry of research, ideation, development and refinement into a finished product. Because of the small size of the last, shoe designers work constantly between two and three dimensions, starting with small thumbnail drawings. A last can be covered in masking tape and a design drawn directly onto the surface after this to see the design in several views. More sketches can be made from drawings made directly onto the last. The key point to remember is that shoes are much smaller than

clothes, so the proportion of the design and scale of components used has to be perfectly functional and have the right aesthetic for the style. Heel shapes must be fully explored as they can be used to make strong design statements, such as the Saint Laurent Opyum Pump with its signature logo heel, or the Cube Shoe by United Nude.

The specialist nature of footwear demands that some designers focus on specific elements of the shoe. For example, in trainers the intricate cutting and branding of the **upper** (top part of the shoe covering the foot) requires one set of skills, while the technology of the **sole** unit (the part of the shoe walked on) requires others.

As with bags, shoes have different construction techniques and seams. A very similar process to that used for bags is gone through to produce technical

specs and tech packs so patterns and materials can be cut and the upper stitched together before it is put onto a last and assembled. Heels are then added, and finally the sole is attached.

The small size of a shoe dictates that a designer must utilize every ounce of creativity to use all its elements as a design opportunity. The initial last shape and heel will give a shoe a contemporary and innovative profile. Materials will fulfil the practical constraints of shoe making and enhance the design through colour and surface texture. Areas like the lining and **sock** can be exploited to add exciting accent colours. Decorative elements can also be added to soles and heels to make a shoe very recognizable, like the signature Louboutin red-soled shoes.

Hardware for shoes is closer to the scale of jewellery than hardware used on clothing or bags. The right scale of hardware will add to the success of a design and is often branded, like the instantly recognizable Gucci double G signature hardware used on many of its shoes.

Footwear has not escaped the gaze of technology. Companies like Prevolve (that make Code footwear) have spearheaded the barefoot movement to provide minimalist shoes that allow feet to move in a natural way. Prevolve uses BioFusion technology to create bespoke, flexible 3D printed shoes based on data of an individual's feet.

Designer Iris van Herpen (b. 1984), known for her 3D printed clothes, and architect Zaha Hadid (1950–2016), both imagined entirely 3D printed collections of wearable and zero-waste shoes as part of a collaboration with United Nude in 2012 and 2013. Each pair was created using hard nylon for the soles and a softer, more flexible thermoplastic polyurethane for the uppers. As less waste was produced than cutting pattern pieces out of leather, the shoes offered a more sustainable option over traditional footwear manufacturing methods.

The environmental impact of shoes comes from the manufacturing stages. Large amounts of machinery powered by fossil fuels are used in the process. On average, the production of one pair of typical running shoes produces 13.6 kg (30 lbs) of carbon dioxide. Chemical adhesives are also used in different parts of shoes, and these can easily leak into the environment through toxic wastewater discharge from the factories. Disposal, the last stage in the life cycle of shoes, also contributes to the environmental impacts of the shoe industry. Once shoes are thrown away, chemicals used in their manufacturing slowly leak into the soil as the shoes decompose.

Christian Louboutin red-soled pumps

Gucci mules with double G hardware detail

Bio1 3D printed trainers by Code

Eyewear

It is estimated that more than 60 per cent of people will wear glasses at some point in their lives, so for many eyewear performs a necessary day-to-day function. Since the birth of eyewear as a cool extra fashion accessory in the mid twentieth century, the popularity of eyewear has escalated through the introduction of designer frames for prescription lenses, sunglasses, sportswear and, increasingly, protective screen glasses.

Like shoes, styles of eyewear reflect different eras and follow trends in clothing. Eyewear is often synonymous with celebrities, such as Audrey Hepburn in the film *Breakfast at Tiffany's*, pop stars like Elton John, David Bowie and Lady Gaga, and cultural icons like Harry Potter. Every fashion brand now includes a range of eyewear as the final touch to an outfit.

For such a small accessory, eyewear is an individual choice as well as a fashion statement. In order to choose the right eyewear, the most current styles need to be considered, as well as the shape and proportions of the face, eye colour and skin tone. Ultimately, more than any other accessory, eyewear says something about our personality and lifestyle. When designing eyewear, it is vital to take these points into consideration and work with the proportions of the face to ensure eyewear sits comfortably and **lenses** are looked through and not over. There are a multitude of styles for both men and women. There are small differences between men's and women's eyewear: men's eyewear tends to have slightly larger, differently shaped **frames** with a longer bridge because of the differences in facial bones and width between the eyes.

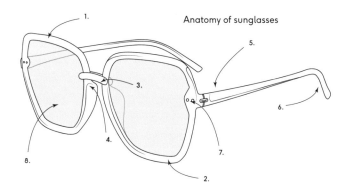
Anatomy of sunglasses

1. Frame – used to secure lenses in front of the wearer's face
2. Full rims – a frame construction that fully surrounds the lens with no gaps; semi-rimmed frames expose half of the lens, usually the lower portion
3. Bridge – the section of the frame that joins the two lenses together and spans across the nose
4. Bridge box – triangular area immediately below the bridge
5. Temple (also known as the 'sides') – attached to the frames by a hinge and reach to each ear
6. Temple drop – the part of the side/temple that hooks round the ear to hold glasses in place
7. Rivets (also called 'pins') – used to permanently fasten the hinges to the frame and temple so the glasses can be folded up or open to be worn
8. Glazing – the lens attachment to the frame

3D printed shoes by Zaha Hadid in collaboration with United Nude

3D printed shoes by Iris van Herpen in collaboration with United Nude

The best way to start designing eyewear is to create a template that fits the standard dimensions of the face. The template should show the front view of the lenses and the side view of the **temple** (side) and **temple drop** (hook round the ear). Once the template is completed it can be printed multiple times and design ideas drawn on top. There are a number of areas that need to be considered, first of which is the shape of the frame – round, oval, cat's eye or geometric. Usually eyewear frames, which are made from metal, plastic or nylon, are symmetrical and, as with footwear, a few millimetres extra and the eyewear may not sit as it should. There are examples of eyewear that have asymmetrical frames with differences usually at the top of the frame. The shape and width of the frame should relate to the temple; thicker frames usually attach to a thicker temple for practical and aesthetic reasons.

Branding is also frequently placed on the temple, so it needs to be wide enough to accommodate this.

The image below demonstrates the main styles for eyewear.

The colour of frames and lenses should relate to each other, particularly when designing sunglasses. Some examples are a dark frame and lenses; a dark frame and tinted lenses; a clear frame and lenses; a textural frame (like tortoiseshell effect) with clear, dark or tinted lenses. The **bridge** (area across the nose linking each lens) and the **bridge box** (area immediately below the bridge) should be decided so frames will not slip down the face. Lens colours are unlimited but some are more suited for general use, such as grey, brown or blue, and some, like the mirrored lens, are more directional and suited for fashion items.

Different eyewear frames

Different tinted lenses

Hardware on eyewear has the practical function of pinning the frames together and hinging the sides. Depending on the construction of the frames, hardware can be visible or discreet. Eyewear is small but different materials such as metal, plastic, nylon, leather and wood can be incorporated into the frames and temples.

Technology, too, has found its place in the development of eyewear, to define personality by incorporating handcrafted details such as patterns and embellishments through personalized 3D printed frames. Sustainable materials are being recycled to create frames for eyewear from materials such as reclaimed cork, wood and bamboo. Bamboo is the fastest growing wood in the world and an excellent material for eyewear because of its strength, lightness and durability. Ray-Ban®, hailed

as the most innovative eyewear brand because of its high-quality polarized lenses that prevent light glare from hitting directly in the eye, created classic styles like the Wayfarer, Aviator and Browline (lenses suspended from the top of the frame), which have become iconic global standards. Sport brands like Oakley® and ROKA have aligned performance eyewear with streetwear. New technology is enabling virtual eyewear to be tried on at home or via phone apps. This makes eyewear even more accessible, so the future of fashion eyewear is set to grow.

ROKA performance sunglasses

Gloves

Originally gloves were considered small leather goods as they were kept in a handbag, but for a time this ladylike accessory denoting social status lost favour for everyday use as both men and women became less bound by formal dress codes. The seasonal and functional nature of gloves has, however, kept them in the spotlight and they are now established in fashion collections as important accessories.

Gloves as fashion accessories can be categorized as either bespoke, mass-produced or luxury. Fine leather gloves made by traditional master craftsmen using craft skills honed over many years, service a growing bespoke market. Mass-produced wider ranges of gloves as fashion accessories include knitted gloves, bridal and evening gloves, and fashion sportswear. High-profile luxury brands have fuelled interest in gloves through a strong catwalk presence.

Gloves come in a wide variety of sizes and different materials, including leather, cotton and wool. Styles vary enormously and can be short wrist length, three-quarter length or full arm length. Because of the anatomy and dexterity of the human hand, the relationship between materials and the fit of the gloves is particularly relevant. Materials will largely determine the fit by the amount of stretch they have and the way in which the gloves are constructed.

The small area of the hand offers few opportunities to make a design statement so when designing gloves it is important to consider ways to use colour, for example between the fingers, to add texture through decorative stitching and embroidery, and to use leather punching (making small decorative

holes). Glove design needs to consider the asymmetry of the hand, how the hand sits against the body, left and right design, and the front and back of a glove.

Jean Paul Gaultier outfit with gloves, S/S 2020

Moschino matching outfit and gloves, A/W 2019/20

Anatomy of a glove

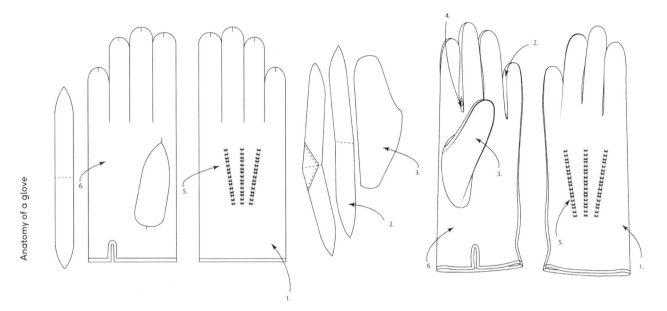

1.   Trank – the main area of the glove across the hand, considered to be the front; when the glove is worn and the hand is by the body the trank faces outwards

2.   Fourchette – the gusset running between each finger of the glove to accommodate movement and allow space for the fingers

3.   Thumb piece – a folded piece that is stitched and inserted into the main glove pattern to allow for mobility of the thumb

4.   Quirk – a tiny square gusset at the bottom of the finger stitched to the fourchette to give more flexibility and a better fit between the fingers

Traditional leather glove construction is at the pinnacle of glove making. It requires very thin leather that is stretched before the glove pattern pieces can be cut and cannot be used for shoes, bags or belts. Traditional leather gloves are made using the finest of materials and the size of stitching indicates the quality of the gloves. Before the construction of a pair of gloves it is necessary to make a pattern that allows for the length of the fingers and size of the palm and that fits close enough to the hand but still allows some tolerance so the glove can be put on and taken off. Individual gloves made by master glove makers use a specific draft for each pattern, whereas standard patterns are used for mass manufacture.

Gloves are essentially constructed using raw-edged seams on the outside or turned seams; functionally because of the fine nature of glove leather and stylistically to create a refined look. The **trank** (top of the hand) traditionally has three lines of raised stitching but also includes punching details with holes cut in the leather. Contrasting colours can be used to highlight the **fourchettes** (gussets between the fingers), which are stitched in as separate pieces. Fittings and hardware for gloves are minimal; occasionally zips, buttons, lacing, eyelets and buckles are used, which should be proportionate to the hand.

It is important to reflect on the purpose of the gloves and any new relevant innovations. For example, UV protection is now used in glove materials to protect the hands from sun damage and leathers that work with smartphone touchscreens are also being used. Although influenced by trends to a lesser degree than clothing and other accessories, glove design can still be influenced by trend cycles. The growth in sportswear, for example, has seen the development of sporty fingerless gloves taking styling influences from cycling, golf or driving gloves. Bold coloured statement gloves, perceived as 'arm adornment', which match shoes and contrast with bags, have also emerged to make sure this once overlooked accessory stands out.

Marc Jacobs perforated leather gloves and matching bag, S/S 2019

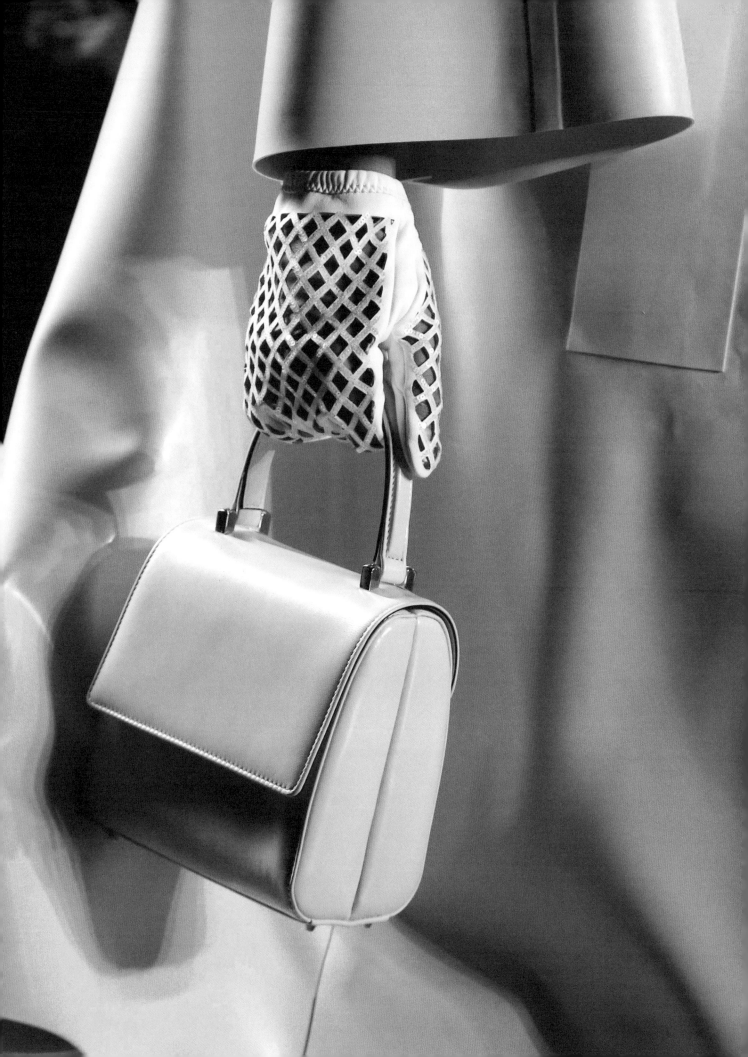

Belts

Every few years the belt is resurrected as a fashion item. At its most basic a belt is nothing more than a strip of material that ties, buckles or fastens around the waist, hips or midriff. The beauty of a belt lies in its width; it can be a barely seen, skinny micro-belt, a broad corset-like belt that cinches the waist creating an hourglass silhouette, or a soft obi-style sash (sash worn around the waist of a Japanese kimono). Thin or thick belts can make a strong statement.

Black leather belt with polished edge

Chanel double C and silver chain belt

Like many accessories, belts serve both a decorative and a functional purpose; they can be used to hold a garment in place or change its outline. Belts can blend in with clothing or be used as accent pieces in bright or contrasting colours to make them stand out. They have bridged the gap between science and fashion through smart belts offering health benefits to wearers (see page 138).

As with shoes and bags, there is a relationship between a belt and clothing. A successful belt design is the correct width in relation to the clothing it is worn with and can be made in many materials, including leather, woven textiles and knitted fabrics.

Traditionally leather belts are made using either a cut raw edge along the length of the belt or a skived and folded edge. Textile belts can be woven, crocheted or knitted materials. Or they can be made from metal links, like those made popular in the 1960s by designers such as Mary Quant.

Whether a belt is made from a beautiful piece of oak-tanned hand-cut leather with custom-made hardware or a crochet textile construction that is tied, it must relate to the overall concept for a range. It must allow the design signature of a brand or particular collection to be visible through its shape, materials and hardware.

Wide obi-style leather belt with silver ring- tie feature

Materials for a belt should be selected so they relate to the function of the belt. Does the belt match a particular piece of clothing? Jeans, for example, originated as workwear and as working men could not afford a tailor to make their trousers fit perfectly, they needed a belt to hold them up. Collaborations between belt makers and jeans companies continue to this day.

There may be particular requirements in terms of the width and style of the belt. All of these should be explored through the processes of sketching ideas and developing shapes. A fundamental decision has to be taken about the ergonomics of the belt. A straight strip of leather sits on the natural waist point but a curved belt takes on the shape of the body and has more natural resting places on the human form. Once materials and shape have been explored, edge treatments – for example polished, painted or stained edges or turned edges – should be investigated, all of which can use contrast colours or linings.

The important design decision on how the belt will fasten needs to be considered next. Fastenings are an integral part of the overall design and feel of a belt. Buckles come in a variety of materials. Nylon or plastic buckles may fit very well with a sportswear collection, or a luxury range may choose a custom designed buckle made and finished in a particular colour that fits with a range. Mass-produced belts may use a piece of off-the-shelf hardware. Whatever hardware is selected, belts should be made in the correct width to fit the hardware. Belt hardware is an important area to showcase innovative branding as well as having the ability to function as a closure, for example the Hermès H buckle or the circular buckles used by Paco Rabanne. Buckles undergo constant use, being done up and undone, so they must be able to withstand daily use and generally come in a few different sizes. Buckles also have the function of adjusting belts to fit three or four different waist sizes comfortably in one belt.

8
Professional Development

The fashion industry is competitive and overcrowded, so to get noticed you need to be more than a talented designer. You need to possess not only the creative vision and design skills but also the personal qualities that will help you to succeed. Successful designers empower themselves through a toolbox of skills, which is constantly updated throughout their professional lives. They require the curiosity to want to learn new things and have the creativity to know how to apply them in original ways. No matter what level of the market, designers must approach design briefs with an open mind to give of their creative best, whether they are entrepreneurs, brand developers or intrapreneurs who bring a unique perspective to an existing company to lead innovations.

What Makes a Successful Designer?

The fashion industry requires certain attributes of a designer, beginning with an honest self-assessment of what they have to offer that is new and relevant and differentiates them. In the competitive world of fashion, creativity is intermeshed with identity so criticism of creative ideas can be uncomfortable and difficult to accept. As a result, designers need to develop a high level of self-awareness and self-criticism. The following questions will help you to decide on your strengths and weaknesses and determine if you have the personal qualities to succeed.

- Do you have confidence in your abilities as a designer?
- Do you have the ability to respond positively in different situations?
- Do you have the resilience to remain self-motivated in the face of uncertainty and rejection of your ideas?
- Do you have the drive and determination to lead a task and see it successfully resolved?
- Are you open to new ideas, new challenges and rapid changes?

Remember that before you enter a position you do not have to be an 'expert' on everything, but you must demonstrate the willingness to learn things you do not know.

As a designer drives the creative direction of a collection, another vital attribute is that they can communicate a clear vision to inspire others. This can be done through visuals or a verbal presentation, and mastering both is a necessary skill in order to present a shared creative vision. A designer may have direct responsibility for turning an idea into a finished product so confidence in the ability to formulate a viable concept and to take calculated risks to realize it are important.

Design is collaborative, so the ability to work alongside others is also essential. Other creatives may not share a designer's vision or may reject their ideas. Being resourceful and responsive to feedback helps push designers beyond creative complacency to find new solutions. This will require negotiation, compromise and acceptance when an idea does not make it off the drawing board. Collaborating with other creatives connects designers to a network of talented people and allows them to contribute to wider communities of practice.

More than anything a successful designer is a catalyst; they create and speed up change to be predictive, agile thinkers. Originality requires feeding through inquisitiveness and the research skills to uncover interesting inspirations and reinterpret information. A designer must generate enthusiasm to seek out new perspectives by building a vast knowledge of contemporary global culture and developing the ability to synthesize information into ideas relevant to accessories design.

Design Education

Every journey to become a designer is different, no matter if you are starting out as a designer or a professional changing direction towards a career in fashion. A design education helps you to decide who you are as a designer and the areas of design you find most stimulating. Fashion accessories design courses are highly specialized to build the basic blocks of knowledge designers need. Research skills, an understanding of colour and shape, drawing skills (both hand and CAD), familiarity with different materials, pattern cutting, sewing skills, specialist techniques and the ability to source components can all be consolidated over a period of study, typically three or four years. Along with this, designers learn how to spot and interpret trends influencing accessories design and create new design directions. Most design courses involve live industry projects, which provide a taste of working to an industry brief, and the opportunity to put forward innovative solutions through design competitions.

Education can make good designers become outstanding, highly qualified designers. Some fashion design degrees combine marketing and business skills for those who intend to start their own design labels or businesses. Apart from learning a craft, a professional training at a prestigious design school adds credibility to a designer in this highly competitive and very selective industry.

The majority of people who study fashion want to be clothing designers; there are fewer accessories design courses and fewer specialist accessories designers trained each year but just as many opportunities in the industry. As a product category, fashion bags and accessories are a highly profitable growth area essential to many brands. There are opportunities for designers who will be immersed in fashion culture but have the opportunity to specialize in a niche area that spans creative fashion design and product design.

Internships

It is useful to do a period of work experience within the fashion industry and this can often be undertaken as part of a course. An internship allows a designer to apply what they have learned through education in a 'real world' situation and helps them focus on a career direction or aspect of the industry they may be less familiar with, for example product development, merchandising or styling. During an internship a designer learns the commercial process of design and manufacture and is also introduced to aspects of accessories design and product development of fashion bags, luggage, small leather goods, gloves, belts and eyewear. This will almost certainly involve working alongside clothing designers who create a wide range of different apparel, including casual wear, sportswear, evening wear and outerwear, that will relate to ranges of bags and accessories. A design role may also include footwear design, creating different styles of shoes and boots, using new materials and combining design flair with comfort, form and function. In some companies or brands, accessories designers also design hardware or work collaboratively with other specialists to develop components.

During an internship a designer undergoes professional development, making them more employable and enabling them to build valuable industry connections. Due to the global nature of the industry, work experience with global fashion companies should be considered to gain exposure to prestigious international brands who may be potential employers. The right internship can introduce a designer to fashion luminaries, who may offer valuable mentorship or share their experiences of the industry. At larger companies, the hands-on work and practical experience might be less, but may provide greater opportunities to network. Smaller start-ups or companies may offer a more rounded experience. An internship should be considered as a relationship benefitting both the intern and the company.

Maison Peaux Neuves grape leather
Haut les Coeurs shoulder bag

The Portfolio

Whether you are applying for a course or a job in the industry it is necessary to create a portfolio of work that represents your best possible face as a designer. At an initial stage it is essential to answer the following questions:

- Who is the portfolio for?
- How will the portfolio reflect your skill set?
- Does the portfolio match the job role applied for?
- What is the best format for your portfolio (digital or physical, landscape or portrait)?

To build an impressive portfolio, a designer should first research presentations of work generally and identify which layouts and graphics are visually interesting and why. For example, the use of direction in a layout, the choice of background colour, the placement of images and text and the scale of images. The aim of a portfolio is to show off a designer's strengths, sense of the aesthetic, proportion and balance, and understanding of communication and collaborations. Strong presentation skills persuade the viewer to engage and take in more information.

A portfolio is a visual representation of a designer's design work and skills and should be thought of as a book. It should have an exciting front cover that makes a viewer want to look inside. It should tell a complete and compelling story, with a contents page, chapter headings, illustrations, and a memorable, stunning last chapter. In order to make sense there must be no pages missing.

A portfolio is of most value when a designer is trying to gain an internship or a first job. Because the designer has no track record or work history in a chosen field on which to be judged, employers will use a portfolio as an indication of what their potential might be. The portfolio represents an invaluable opportunity for a designer to sell themselves to companies or industrial specialists. If applying for a particular role, the portfolio must match with the requirements needed to fulfil that role. A design role reflects all aspects of design, and the portfolio should include hand and CAD drawing. A product development role will focus on the process of making prototypes and the portfolio should include more use of CAD technical illustrations. If you are applying for different roles, it is better to create different portfolios reflecting each role. It is not essential to produce all your visual work on a computer, but it is important your portfolio shows you have mastered industry essentials like Photoshop and Illustrator CAD software.

Putting together a successful portfolio follows a series of steps and requires appraisal, analysis and editing of work and skills with a critical eye. Competition within the fashion industry is fierce and there will be many graduates and young designers looking for internships or job opportunities who have excellent portfolios.

Creating a Portfolio

A portfolio should primarily use visuals, drawings, pictures and photography to tell a rounded visual story about a designer. For example, including sketchbook pages will show thought processes and how an idea is developed, and a finished layout will show the fully resolved ideas. Both types of drawing show skills that communicate ideas effectively at different stages of the design process.

Once you have decided on your focus, remind yourself of the job description or the role you are applying for to make sure the skills shown in the portfolio match. When your portfolio is viewed there is a short time to make an impression, so it must be relevant and reflect what a potential employer is looking for. Designers are sometimes asked by a brand to create a specific portfolio project for them. Doing your homework to find out about the brand's history, key employees, product ranges, key markets, consumers and collaborations, as well as any focus on particular initiatives such as philanthropy, sustainable practice or new innovations, can inform the style and content of the portfolio project. Any portfolio project should contain the essence of a brand and clearly demonstrate an understanding of it. The portfolio should seek to advance the brand's current position. No designer has ever been employed to tell a brand what they already know or to design products they are already selling.

Canvas and leather bag by Chloe Shinnie

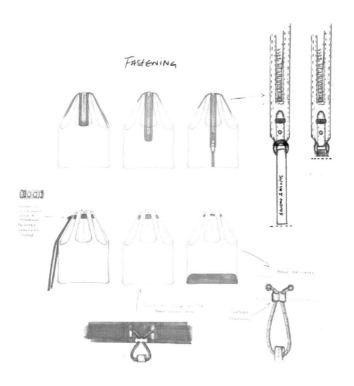

Examples of sketchbook pages, technical drawing by Elleannor Moore

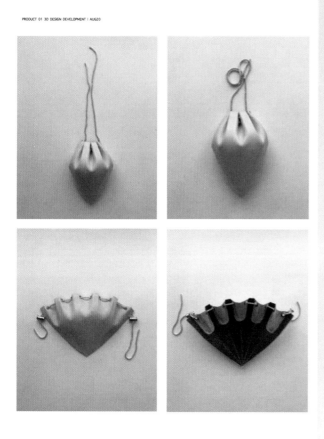

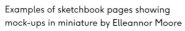

Examples of sketchbook pages showing mock-ups in miniature by Elleannor Moore

Leather bag by Elleannor Moore

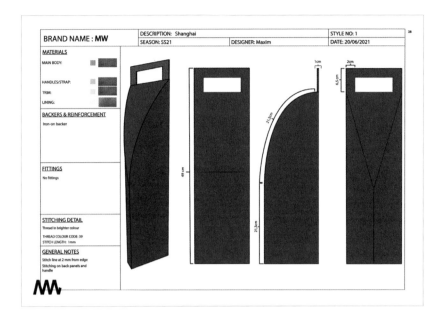

Long leather Champagne bag (opposite)
and technical drawing by Maxim Winckers

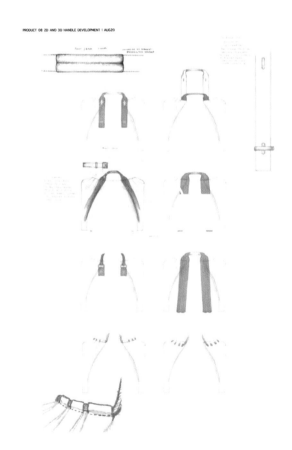

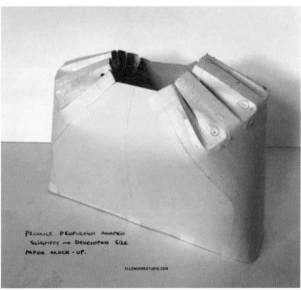

Sketchbook pages and mock-ups in miniature
by Elleannor Moore

CAD images of handbag and interior view
by Annika Andersson

Physical or Digital Portfolio?

Physical and digital portfolios do different things and there are advantages and disadvantages to both. Physical portfolios represent work that does not read well on a screen; the work may be something tactile and textured that needs to be presented physically. Physical work must be portable and easy to present around a desk to several people, so size and the ability to handle the work without difficulty is critical. A well-presented physical portfolio makes it easier to lead viewers through a narrative, keeping a specific order with fewer issues around format. This type of portfolio cannot be shared so easily and thus offers more copyright protection. They can be expensive to produce, however, with high printing costs for professional looking portfolio pages, but are worth the investment for bespoke, handcrafted or detailed tactile work.

Physical portfolios should be a maximum of A3 (tabloid) in size, which is the industry standard size for design portfolios. Showing a portfolio in a crowded or busy office makes anything bigger impractical. Footwear portfolios can be A3 (tabloid) or A4 (letter), but choosing a non-standard size between these can mean a portfolio becomes more visible and stands out from others.

Digital portfolios offer the most ability to customize pages. They can be quickly and widely shared and are inexpensive to produce. Digital illustrations look professional on screen but can look generic if created using the same software and filters. A digital portfolio can be unpredictable and it is important to know how it works and looks when viewed on different devices. The file size of a digital portfolio may become too large to view easily or lose quality if files are compressed incorrectly. It is easier

CAD images of a drawstring pouch bag by Annika Andersson

to view a digital portfolio 'out of sequence' so they should always be submitted as one file. This also makes it simpler to talk through work at an interview where just one document needs to be opened. Presenting a digital portfolio on a tablet in an interview makes it much easier to share than on a laptop but both restrict the size of images. Digital portfolios should be password protected and all pages watermarked and copyrighted so they cannot be downloaded without permission and easily copied. As digital portfolios suffer from 'swipe fatigue' they also need to be more edited than a physical portfolio.

While digital portfolios are a great way to offer a taster of work, physical portfolios can often show more individuality and flair. If you are sending your portfolio to a company a digital version is more convenient, but in face-to-face meetings they are harder to share

because of limited screen size. Moving closer to a piece of paper rather than zooming in on a presentation seems a more natural way to view ideas. A physical portfolio may be an easier experience in an interview, but the decision still has to be an individual one and may depend on how work has been produced in the first instance and how well the quality of physical work can be represented on a screen. 3D visualization software will further impact portfolio presentation to show design skills and the mastery of relevant CAD software to realize realistic products which surpass physical drawings or 2D CAD rendered images. 3D visualization images can be used in both physical and digital portfolios.

Both digital and physical portfolios can be read as either landscape (laptops) or portrait (tablets and phones). A common mistake is to mix formats. From a practical point of view it is easier to show work if it is

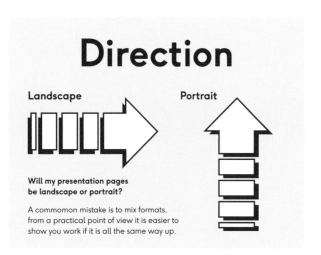

Directional design and page layout by
Darla-Jane Gilroy

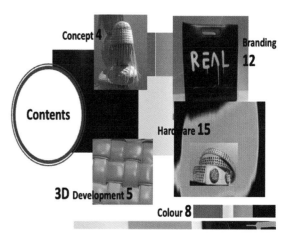

Example of a visual contents page by
Darla-Jane Gilroy

all the same way up in the portfolio. Most design work can be naturally divided up into projects and it makes sense to reflect this in a portfolio. It is also easier to talk through work if you create some natural breaks and pauses.

Using Graphics

Viewers lose interest in portfolios quickly if they do not see what they want straight away and may make a snap decision about a designer's worth. Only the strongest work should be included and, if in doubt, show less work but of the highest quality. Using graphic elements, such as backgrounds, lettering and different scale drawings, is a valuable way to create visual drama and keep viewers visually stimulated. Colourful backgrounds can focus attention on design work. Select backgrounds that are sympathetic to the work and create a theme or relationship that runs through the projects or portfolio. The same is true of typefaces. Choose lettering that is easy to read and has some sympathy with the design work. Typefaces also follow trends and using out of date ones will make a portfolio appear tired and old fashioned. The scale of drawings, images and lettering is also important and a useful means of creating visual impact.

For example, thumbnail sketches can be combined with larger photographs, illustrations or text to produce an exciting layout.

Plan in Miniature

Putting together a portfolio can be a lot of work; making a plan in miniature before starting allows for experimentation and will focus time and resources effectively. There are no hard and fast rules to portfolio presentation but there are basic rules of graphic design that are worth following to create a professional portfolio.

Not all images have the same impact, so it is vital to establish the hierarchy of images on a page and make the most important images bigger. Decide on whether your layouts will be symmetrical or asymmetrical. Symmetrical layouts are balanced, using set design elements from left to right or top to bottom. Asymmetrical layouts create a balanced layout without using symmetry, and rely heavily on visual hierarchy and scale. They create visual drama and dynamic directional layouts that lead the eye across the page.

Miniature sketchbook planning
by Sebastian Mendoza Gutierrez

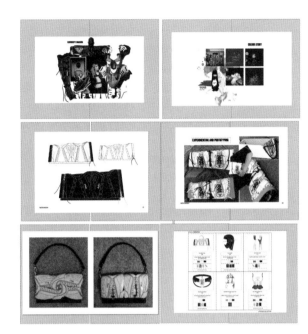

Digital portfolio
– Direction
– Relationship
  between image
  and text
– Images per page
– Scale change

What's your story?
– Concept
– Design ideas
– Edits
– Details
– Materials
– Techniques
– Colour
– Audience

Symmetrical layouts

Asymmetrical layouts

Consistent backgrounds

Top to bottom layouts

CAD image of a hand-held bag by Holly Cowan

The use of images that sit in pairs or groups that complement each other is effective in portfolio presentation. For example, using two pictures from the same photoshoot or using images that all share the same mood and aesthetic.

Within one design project it is important to use similar coloured backgrounds or filters when printing out images, and in a digital portfolio it is important to think about breaking up the default white background. Use of high-contrast colours helps elements stand out or draws attention to design features, and repeating elements creates a sense of consistency. For example, three different projects shown within a single portfolio would require each project to be given a visual identity by applying specific elements and styles of graphics and

typography. Use of space can also be powerful and effective. Leaving empty space around an image can make it more noticeable and using space strategically within a portfolio can provide clarity to images and layouts.

One of the most important graphic rules is the alignment of images on the page achieved by imagining a border all the way round the page. Professional and consistent page layouts are created by making sure images sit within this border. This is easily done when using CAD software like Illustrator but more difficult with a physical portfolio. Perhaps the simplest graphic rule to remember is the rule of thirds, where each page is divided into three rows and three columns. Wherever lines meet, focal points are created.

Expand Your Horizons

A key element of success for a designer is the ability to challenge themself to go beyond their comfort zone. Branching out into wider designer communities beyond the discipline of fashion brings rewards. The challenge of working with designers who may think and work in very different ways enables a designer to evaluate and develop their own practice to become more original and innovative, and helps to support creative collaborations.

Scope luggage by Marc Newson for Samsonite

Industrial designer Marc Newson (b. 1963) has collaborated with luggage brand Samsonite and luxury fashion brand Louis Vuitton to create luggage ranges in pioneering new materials. Through experimenting with thermoplastic foams and laminating different materials together, Newson created a revolutionary lightweight, durable and strong knitted material, which was neither soft nor hard, to design the Scope range of luggage in 2005. Following this he developed with Louis Vuitton a range of innovative rolling soft luggage for contemporary travellers made from 3D synthetic knitted fabric featuring his interpretation of Louis Vuitton's signature monogram. The custom-made technical fabric uses seamless knitting technology and creates no waste.

Through activism within the fashion industry, issues of overconsumption, waste and inequality are currently being discussed. Initiatives like the Green Carpet awards have seen designers and celebrities globally bring the best of sustainable fashion to the awards season. The Parley Ocean Plastic initiative, which has created a space for creatives to come

Troubadour Weekender

together to raise awareness of plastic pollution (see page 103), and the commitment of French luxury goods company Kering to carbon neutrality across its supply chain, including its fashion houses Balenciaga, Gucci, Saint Laurent and Alexander McQueen, are both valuable initiatives to engage with when trying to locate your place within the fashion industry.

Specialist industry forums like trade shows provide inspiration, exhibitions and showcases of new ideas, materials and processes. Lineapelle and Première Vision Leather and Accessories are shows where designers can source materials, hardware and components for new collections of accessories and make contacts within the industry. Trade shows, such as MAGIC Las Vegas, Texworld Paris and USA, MICAM Milano, International Apparel & Textile Fair, Intertextile Shanghai Apparel Fabrics, Chandigarh Mega Expo, East China Fair and Pure London, are selling shows where new collections are shown to buyers, and also offer the chance to network and become part of the wider fashion community.

In the new digital landscape, the future of trade shows will include more virtual events that are convenient, cost effective and sustainable.

Brand You

Networking is an important part of expanding your horizons to enhance professional opportunities. It is also a good way to align yourself with other professionals who share your interests and values, which can be explored through the concept of personal branding.

More than any other industry, the fashion industry creates a focus on individuals with specific qualities. When we think of brands we automatically think of big companies and branded products, but anything can be a brand. An individual can have a personal brand that influences our perceptions of them and establishes and promotes what they stand for. A personal brand is the unique combination of skills and experiences that make an individual original and differentiates them from others in their field. Personal brands exist both online and offline and are important professionally because they offer a chance to combine a distinct personal identity with a like-minded company or brand.

Social media platforms amplify personal branding, creating an opportunity to control a personal brand narrative. Something of your individual voice and personality should show through in the things you do, which will make you memorable. Building a personal brand requires a strategic approach to the effective use of social media platforms in order to cross-promote and build a network of industry insiders and global connections. In a career sense, personal branding allows you to develop a career strategy and align your goals with the company you work for or gauge your success based on your individual goals.

Gucci S/S 2018

Pathway to Success

Breaking into the fashion industry can seem daunting; talent and connections will help but a strategic approach is essential. There are many areas to work in so the first thing to decide is whether you want to work for a company or brand or if you want to work for yourself. Then you will have to decide on the level of the market you are most fervent about. Do you have a passion for one-off bespoke craft making or high street ready-to-wear? Do you want to create slow fashion models or design for a purpose to solve a particular problem?

Deciding whether you want to work for a company or work for yourself is a big decision with pros and cons to each. When starting out, working within a company provides experience, mentorship, the chance to make connections and the certainty of a wage packet each month. Self-employment offers more creative control and flexibility in working but comes with the sole responsibility for a company and any employees and a steep learning curve to accumulate knowledge and experience to create a viable business. Freelance working as an alternative to being an employee or starting a business can be rewarding because it offers freedom to set your own schedule of where and when to work, more flexibility in the work you do, and new opportunities and independence. A more digitized global economy is offering alternative ways of working that go beyond geographical boundaries. As a freelancer you may have more autonomy than a permanent employee, but that comes at a price and may mean fewer legal rights and less control over workflow. You may be very busy during certain times and less busy at others, affecting how much you earn and when. As a freelancer you will also need to network and to build connections to ensure your work opportunities remain current.

If initially you want to work for a brand, make a list of the people and companies you would most like to work for or most aspire to emulate. Undertake detailed, diligent research to make sure you have the most current information and contacts. You can make initial contact through professional social media platforms, if appropriate, as a way to introduce yourself and your ambition to work for the company or brand. You may only get one opportunity to make contact so be cautious and well informed. In covering letters and job applications be honest about your previous experience and well versed in the job description so that you can tailor your previous experience to match it. Your curriculum vitae (CV) should include a 'raison d'être' in the form of a personal statement that explains who you are creatively and what your design ethos is. You should know what you can bring to the role that the other candidates cannot, how you can contribute to the success of the company, and what you hope to learn in return. Make sure all information is clear and concise and your contacts and references are kept up to date. Include relevant links to endorsements, social media platforms or a digital portfolio of work if required.

The next stage may well be an interview and you will need to prepare for this by researching the brand or company thoroughly and anticipating likely questions. You should be able to summarize your CV so you can talk confidently about yourself, highlighting anything relevant to the job role you are applying for. Questions around your strengths are often asked, for example how you would deal with a missed deadline. Or ones that focus on specific technical skills, such as which CAD software packages you can use. You may also be asked competency-based questions that test a specific skill. For example, you may be asked to describe a situation in which you have worked successfully as part of a team. However much you prepare there may always be unforeseen questions so be ready for the unexpected. You should also have questions ready to ask your interviewers that will help you find out more about the job role and the company, and ask for the next steps so you are clear what will happen after the interview.

If you want to start a business you need to be businesslike, but this does not mean you need to know everything about running a business or be a financial expert. You will need to be business savvy enough to present yourself and your business concept to potential investors or business partners. The first question you will be asked is about how your product range is different from competitor brands and, if you have spotted a niche market, whether the market is big enough for your product to be grown into a sizable business. A fulfilling hobby is not the same as a scalable business. Choose financial investors with care and take legal and financial advice before entering into legal contracts. Study brands or businesses, some of which may be outside of fashion, who have been successful and create case studies to help you to make a sound financial plan and business case.

If at First You Don't Succeed

In the case of the fashion industry, few designers have overnight success. Their successes are built on their creative capital, hard work, diligence, determination, commitment and passion. If you are unsuccessful in a job application, ask for feedback and use it to help sharpen the skills needed to succeed in the future. Keep in contact with Human Resources (HR) departments to find out about future roles that may be advertised. Be prepared to travel as fashion is a global industry. Send out a digital 'taster' portfolio of work to generate interest in your work, promote your personal brand in an authentic way, and try to build contacts within companies you want to work for. Specialist fashion recruiters place designers within the fashion industry and can give valuable advice about how to improve a portfolio or CV and interview techniques. They will give a designer all the benefit of their industry knowledge and experience. Their industry connections have been gained through running successful recruitment businesses, so it is well worth registering with them. Remember, persistence pays off.

What Can You Expect from Your First Job?

A designer will create original designs for fashion bags and other accessories. They research, sketch designs, select materials and patterns, and give instructions on how to make the products they design. Larger companies often employ teams of designers headed by a creative director. Each team will specialize in one product category, for example clothing, footwear or accessories design, which is then broken down into styles like casualwear or outerwear.

Accessories designers typically do the following:

- Research trends and use them to anticipate design directions that will appeal to consumers
- Decide on a theme or concept for a collection
- Use hand drawing and CAD programs to create designs
- Visit manufacturers or trade shows to get samples of materials and components
- Select materials, embellishments, colours, etc., for each style of accessory
- Work with other designers or team members to create prototypes and sample designs
- Present design ideas to creative directors or showcase their ideas in fashion or trade shows
- Oversee the final production of their designs

3D printed bag Ruby's Last Stone
by Vienna-based brand Published By

INTERVIEW: Alexandra Klimek

'Designers need a strong sense of self-belief. My advice would be to never stop believing in yourself, nobody cares about your career as much as you do.'

Alexandra Klimek

Alexandra Klimek is a graduate of the BA Cordwainers Fashion Accessories design course at the London College of Fashion, and was the winner of the Best Handbag in Overall Style and Design in the Independent Handbag Designer Awards 2020.

Since graduating Klimek has worked for Alexander McQueen, Anya Hindmarch and Mulberry as an accessories designer. She always wanted to start her own fashion accessories label, but first wanted to gain more knowledge of craft making, pattern cutting and product development, and acquire the commercial experience to help her to start a business and be successful in establishing her brand.

Why did you decide to study accessories design?

I had a strong interest in industrial design but also in fashion, and I could not decide between the two courses, so I decided to study both degrees at the same time. After a year I realized that although I was very interested in fashion, I preferred working on smaller scale objects and enjoyed the challenge of working in a range of different materials and processes. Having to solve both aesthetic and practical problems in one item to find the balance between form and function was interesting and a constant stimulus.

My tutors suggested that I should consider accessories design and, after doing some research, I found my way from my native Poland to the BA Cordwainers Fashion Accessories course at the London College of Fashion in the UK.

What do you think is the value of an accessories design education and what are the skills you have learned from your course that you have used as a professional designer?

I don't think I could do what I'm doing now without my university education. There are lots of opportunities to learn things online now and it's

tempting to think that you can teach yourself what you need to know, but the mentoring, the creative environment and the exposure to new ideas, techniques and materials was priceless.

My tutors came from a range of different industry backgrounds and guided me through the process of learning to explore myself as a creative person and develop my own design handwriting. The student body was international, so I gained a broad perspective on global design.

In my first year the course underpinned my knowledge of accessories design by teaching me the fundamentals of research, design development, pattern cutting and working in leather and other materials to create products. As I progressed, I gained confidence and more knowledge. My course has established links with industry, so I was able to make connections to do an internship at the end of my second year. Doing my internship was the greatest thing ever because it enabled me to put everything I learnt at university into a real-life industry context. When you're a student you worry about what you don't know, but my internship built my confidence to know I had many skills that were valuable to industry, like research skills, creative design and CAD skills. I learnt a lot about sourcing materials and hardware, technical drawing and the design cycle from my internship, and gained the management skills to navigate my final year at university. I would never have reached the same level of understanding and professionalism without having gone to university and it demonstrated to my employers that I could commit to something for a period of years and see it all the way through.

What do you think are the personal attributes that have made you successful?

If you pursue a career in finance there can be a hundred vacancies in one company for graduates and thousands of entry-level jobs each year. The fashion industry is not as straightforward; for accessories designers there are fewer entry-level positions each year so it's tempting to take any position offered. It can take longer to find your ideal job with a company you really want to work for so my determination and the resilience to find the right position as opposed to *any* position definitely paid off. Looking back, there are jobs I didn't get but with hindsight I am glad I didn't get them; they weren't the right jobs for me and didn't reflect my strengths or skill set. I aimed high and managed to get jobs I really wanted. I was able to fit into different teams and build positive relationships with colleagues to learn new skills and benefit from

their experiences. I also had to be prepared to compromise my ideas sometimes and be very honest about the things I could do well and the skills I still needed to master.

How do you see the patterns of work changing in the future?

There are many more exciting freelance opportunities now and that's a trend that will continue. We are used to working online so the barriers to being in different countries have been removed. We've acquired digital skills and proved we can work efficiently. Things that were seen as necessary to be done face-to-face can now be done remotely, like checking samples, and we have changed the way we think about working remotely to accommodate increasing reliance on a flexible freelance workforce. That offers a great opportunity to acquire a broad skills base working for a few companies at the same time.

How important do you think it is to define your consumer and market level, and how have you gone about doing this in terms of your own brand?

It is really important to understand the consumer, their needs, their spending habits and their lifestyles, firstly because this determines the product, the design aesthetic, the way it's made, and materials used. More importantly, we are living in countries where we have transient populations and groups of consumers who have very different attitudes to spending money. It has been a very interesting journey to observe consumer behaviour and to have the opportunity to unpack buying habits. Increasingly consumers don't want a click experience online, they want to connect with a product that reflects some of their own values, especially in regard to quality, sustainability and overconsumption. Gathering feedback from customers is an important way to constantly fine-tune what you offer in a range.

Luxury is a word we hear a lot. How would you define luxury and would you apply it to your own products?

Increasingly, we see 'affordable luxury' as a concept that defeats the object of luxury; you cannot have mass-produced bags and present them as luxury items. To me luxury means handcrafted, original, and attention to detail, with a powerful connection and story that consumers can relate to. I produce small production runs that are handmade rather than mass produced. As we shop more and more online, luxury items will reflect a connection with our senses, not just a click-and-buy experience.

What are the main challenges of running your own business and how does this differ from working within a company structure?

You are definitely in a comfort zone when you are working for other people. Now, working for myself, there is a zero-comfort zone. The main differences when I was employed were that my job roles were specific. I was confined to particular areas, for example working within a design team or sourcing fabrics, so it was hard to understand all of the broader activities of the company, for example communication channels through social media, website design, photo shoots and contact with buyers or stores.

Launching my own brand means I have had to become an expert in everything connected with running a successful business. I very quickly had to learn the differences between all the different job roles, like creative direction, art direction and finance, which has been challenging but exciting. One of the greatest challenges has been financing my company and using financial investment wisely. Working for a bigger company means there is always financial support. Now I have to think strategically before I invest money into areas of the business. For example, I have to be very mindful of

the cost of testing ideas and sampling, which is a significant cost to any business.

What's the best piece of advice you would give to someone who is thinking of starting their own business?

Quite often the fear of what you don't know stops you from pursuing your dreams, but inevitably you get to the point where you just have to start after a period of planning and reflection. It is surprising how quickly you learn what you need to know. Designers need a strong sense of self-belief. My advice would be to never stop believing in yourself, nobody cares about your career as much as you do.

What is a typical working day like for you?

I am organized by nature, so I plan my working week and a schedule for each day to know exactly what I have to achieve and any important deadlines to be met. I start every day with my emails, either at home or from my studio, to answer enquiries, deal with suppliers or process orders. My day is always a balance between digital work on my computer, for example drawing designs or technical specifications, and the prototyping I like to do to work out ideas. The nature of accessories design is that it is not a fluid process, so this gives me an opportunity to blend my digital drawing and 3D prototyping.

A key consideration is how to maintain my creative impetus when I have to multitask and turn my attention to so many other areas important for running a business. I make time to travel when I can, and visit exhibitions. I constantly draw ideas down, even if they're not directly relevant to a collection I am currently working on; they may be ideas I will return to in the future. I read a lot of reports on the industry to get a sense of where the industry is going, as many of the decisions I have made have been based on my understanding of the emerging trends in consumer behaviour.

What do you feel will be the balance between physical making and digital visualization?

I don't enjoy digital books. I like to have a physical object in my hand to flick through the pages and read so I feel we will never get to the point where we just produce designs or samples digitally. Different segments of the market, for example luxury, premium or high street, may see more or less digital interventions, particularly where there is little seasonal variation in designs. I read recently that there are around 2 billion items of clothing each year that go unsold, so digital production definitely offers the opportunity to minimize waste in the industry and embed better, more sustainable practices. There is something very appealing and satisfying about hand making which will never completely disappear.

How important is being ethical and sustainable and how do we avoid the trap of overproduction?

Emerging brands have an opportunity to embed sustainable practices by addressing over-consumption and overproduction from the very beginning. We have the opportunity to make made-to-order products and small production runs, particularly by using social media and online sales platforms to gain exposure, while still making a viable business model. Smaller brands have the opportunity to be able to monitor our data to see how items are selling and we can plan our resources and production effectively to make what we know we can sell.

How important do you think seasonality and genderless products will be in the future?

We are moving away from the idea of seasonality; brands usually have two seasons each year and perhaps mid-season drops of new products in between. I think there is a big trend towards making seasonless and timeless pieces that last a long time.

The picture of gendered or non-gendered products is more complex. It is still true to say that, based on consumer needs, women tend to carry more around with them than men, so it is unlikely we will lose the concept of men's and women's bags completely. In my case my brand is for anyone who wants to buy and wear my products.

What advice would you give to a recent graduate, and if you were going to employ an intern what qualities would you look for?

As a recent graduate it's very tempting to apply for any job you see. My advice would be to take more time to find the right opportunities and look at job roles not just in relation to what you can learn, but what you can bring in terms of your own knowledge and experience to advance a company. Research companies and find opportunities that match your design skills and your interests. Don't have a generic portfolio, cover letter and CV because this feels inauthentic to a company and will show at an interview.

Talent is of course important, but I always look for enthusiasm and passion over experience. If you have the desire to learn and do well you are a great asset to a company and will master what you need to learn.

Glossary

Accent colour – Bright colour used in small quantities to draw attention to elements of products in a collection.

Augmented reality – An interactive experience of the real world.

Base colour – Predominant colour used in larger quantity across a collection.

Biodegradable – Ability to decompose naturally without environmental harm.

Bridge – The section of the eyewear frame that joins the lenses together across the nose.

Bridge box – The triangular area immediately below the bridge.

Brief – Instructions developed in consultation with a client or consumers that define the scope and management of a design project.

Butted edges – Folded edges laid next to each other.

Butted seams – A turned seam that is stitched together edge to edge without a seam allowance.

Chrome tanning – A process of tanning leather using chromium salts.

Clochette – a small, bell-shaped covering for keys that is attached to a handbag.

Colour palette – An edited range of colours used across a collection.

Design cycle – The processes designers go through to help them create and evaluate products.

Design for disassembly – Designing products so that elements can be easily removed and reused with minimal environmental impact.

Embossed leather – Stamping a design onto the surface of leather.

Ergonomics – The fit between the body and an object.

Ethical production – The consideration of how products are made, under what conditions and life cycle, in order to create more equitable products and minimize environmental impact.

Expanded view – A diagram or technical drawing of an object, showing its component parts separated out by distance to show construction.

Fair trade – Trade between developing and developed countries, where fair prices are paid for goods produced.

Fourchette – Gussets between each finger of a pair of gloves.

Frame – The structure that holds the lenses in eyewear.

Full-grain leather – Highest-quality of leather with an unpolished surface so it retains its natural characteristics.

Grain – The texture, appearance and composition of a hide or skin.

Gusset – A triangular piece inserted into a seam to add volume or reduce stress on a seam.

Hand skiving – Thinning down areas of leather by hand.

Hardware – Functional and decorative elements of a bag, usually made of metal: these connect straps and handles; close a bag, such as locks and frames; protect bags, such as the metal studs on the base of a bag or metal corners; and branded logo plates.

Heel – A wood or plastic piece attached to the bottom of the shoe to create different heights.

Heel stiffener – Support for the back of the shoe.

Hides – The tanned skin of a large animal such as a cow.

Hue – Different shades of the six primary or secondary colours – yellow, orange, red, violet, blue and green.

Ideation drawings – Small sketches used to capture ideas quickly.

Insole board – A template of the bottom of a shoe.

Kips – Skins made from young animals that are not fully grown.

Last – Three-dimensional representation of a foot around which a shoe is made.

Lenses – Two pieces of glass or plastic that are secured in the frame and sit over each eye.

Microfibres – Very fine tightly woven synthetic yarn.

Mock-up – Experimental model or replica of a product.

Monogrammed – Combining initials of a name to create a decorative logo that conveys identity.

Mood board – Visual summary of research images.

Nap – The fibrous under-side of leather opposite to the smooth grain side.

Nappa leather – A full-grain, unsplit leather that is exceptionally soft and flexible.

Nubuck – Durable with a velvet-like finish. Nubuck is made from the top layer of a hide.

One-piece construction – A pattern piece with a built-in base to create volume.

One-point – A perspective drawing with a single vanishing point placed on a horizon line, used for drawing objects from the front.

Patent leather – Leather with either resin or plastic layer applied to create a shiny surface.

Pattern drafting – Drawing the template pattern pieces that are individually cut and sewn together to make a product.

Perspective drawings – A form of linear drawing that uses lines meeting on a horizon line to realistically represent three-dimensional objects.

Persuasive illustrations – Rendered finished illustrations used to convey the concept of a collection.

Presentation sheets – Fully finished and coloured drawings of products in a collection.

Price range – The range of prices across a collection of products.

Primary research – Research from original sources (you generate yourself).

194

Process sketches – Hand-drawn sketches used to work out and explain a design.

Product development – The process of producing a finished product from a design concept.

Product life cycle – Stages a product goes through, from its development to its decline and disappearance.

Prototype – A full-size and functioning sample of a final product.

Quirk – A small gusset to provide extra flexibility.

Raw edges – Cut, unfinished edges.

Recycle – To reuse waste material to create something new and usable.

Regenerative design – Design and product development processes that restore and renew to promote positive impacts.

Reinforcements – Textiles that are attached to the back of materials to provide strength and stability.

Rendering – Applying colour and textured detail to a drawing.

Reticule – A small decorative drawstring pouch that was used as a handbag by women in the eighteenth and early nineteenth century.

Secondary research – Research taken from existing sources (generated by other people).

Shank – Metal stiffener used to retain the pitch of a high-heeled shoe.

Sides – A hide that has been cut in half.

Signature piece – A distinctive item that conveys the personality and values of a brand.

Signature print – A distinctive print that is used across product categories to convey brand identity.

Skins – The tanned skin of small animals such as sheep or goats

Slow fashion – A way to stem the overproduction and overconsumption of fashion items.

Small leather goods – Items carried in bags that hold objects like coins, keys or credit cards, or protect products like sunglasses or earbuds.

Smart materials – Materials that are changed by external factors like chemicals, heat or electrical impulses.

Sock – A lining inside a shoe.

Sole – The bottom part of a shoe used to cover the internal parts of a shoe.

Splitting – The process of cutting a leather hide or skin into several layers.

Suede – Made from the under-side of a hide or skin, suede has a velvet-like napped finish and soft handle.

Supply chain – A sequence of processes required in order to produce and distribute a product.

Sustainable design – Design processes that reduce the negative impact of design and product development on the environment.

Synthetic materials – Materials made from artificial substances or chemicals.

Tanning – The process of converting animal skins into leather.

Tech pack (technical pack) – A multi-page document that includes precise information in order to make an exact sample.

Technical drawings – Line drawings that convey the design, product function and construction of a product used to create accurate samples.

Temple – Sides of eyewear attached to the frames by hinges.

Temple drop – The part of the temple that is shaped to fit around the ears.

Three-point – Perspective drawing often used for aerial views using three vanishing points, two on the horizon line and one above or below it.

Thumb piece – An insert in a glove to accommodate the thumb.

Toe puff – Support for the front of the shoe.

Tone – Subtle, less vibrant shades of primary and secondary colours.

Trank – Front of a glove.

Turned edges – Cut edges that are turned over and secured.

Turned seams – Raw edges stitched together and then glued or stitched flat.

Two-piece construction – Two equal-sized pattern pieces stitched together like a pencil case.

Two-point – Linear drawing that places two vanishing points on a horizon line and is used for drawing objects in three-quarter view.

Two-tone leather – Leather that has two layers of pigment applied; the top layer is uneven and allows the bottom layer to show through.

Upcycle – To reuse waste material to create a new product of a higher value than the original.

Upper – The top part of the shoe formed around the last.

Vanishing point – A point at which parallel lines meet on a horizon line.

Vegetable (veg) tanning – A process of tanning leather using natural tannins like tree bark.

Virtual reality – A simulated experience similar or different to one from the real world.

Zero waste – Economic and responsible use of resources to eliminate waste.

Zero-waste production – Economic and responsible use of resources to eliminate waste during product development.

Index

Page numbers in *italics* indicate illustration captions.

3D design 134
  3D fabric 183
  3D printing 76, 131, 157, 161
  3D realization tools 73
  3D sampling 116
  3D virtual prototyping 56–7, 84–5, 192
  3D visualization software 68, 69, 80, 82, 139, 179

A

accent colours 63
accessories 9
  belts 166–7
  flat accessories 148–9
  footwear 153–7
  gloves 162–4
  new tech accessories 141–5
  three-dimensional accessories 150–1
  wearable accessory tech 138
acrylic 94
adidas 44, 50, *60*, 103
Adobe 80
  Adobe Creative Suite 84
Alexander McQueen 44, 153, 185, 189
Alexandra Institute, Denmark 136
Alexandra K 109
Anya Hindmarch 189
Apple 144
apple leather 109
ASOS 140
Aspinal of London *149*, *150*
ATLR RSVD 110
augmented reality (AR) 134, 139–40
AutoCAD 85

B

BA Cordwainers Fashion Accessories design course 189–90
backpacks 30, 34
bag charms 147, 150
bags 9, 10–14
  designer bags 15–22

genderless bags 36–8
importance of fashion bags 24
luggage 37–9
men's bags 31–5
women's bags 25–30
baguette bags 28
Balenciaga 26, 29, 185
  Motorcycle bag 22–3
bamboo 14, 161
banana leather 108
Bang & Olufsen 142
Barbour 34, 91
base colours 63
belts 166–7
  WELT belt 138
Berluti 144
Biba 17
biodegradability 87
BioFusion 157
Birkin, Jane 19
  Birkin bag 19, 32, 36, 129
Blender 3D 85
body conscious accessories 151
Bolt Threads *129*
Bottega Veneta 27, 28, 35, 44, 101, 105, 110
BOTTLETOP 96, 127
brand identity 59–60
  brand you 185
briefcases 35
briefs 43
bum bags (fanny packs) 147, 151
Burberry 24, 27, 29, 32, 34, 60–1, 139–40
  Burberry check *63*
butted edges and seams 123

C

cactus leather 108
CAD software 71, 80, 83, 84, 187, 188, 191
  CAD for 3D modelling 85
  CAD for creative design 84
  digital fashion designers 134
  perspective drawings 76
  portfolios 173, 179, 182
  technical drawings 73

Cambridge Satchel Co. 30
card holders 148
Celine 26, 91, 142
Chanel 19, 24, 36, 101, *105*, 156, 166
  Chanel, Coco 13, 15, 19
charger cases 144, 147
Cher 17
Chloé 22, 44
Christian Louboutin 62, *153*, 156
chrome tanning 100–1
Clemens, Telfar 38
CLO3D 85
clutch bags 27
Coach 24, 28, 150
coin purses 150
colour 62–3
  colour palettes 52
Comme des Garçons 30, 35, 92
concepts 50
construction 116–17
  assembly 124
  edging and seams 122–3
  equipment basics 118
  final sample 125
  first sample 120–1
  multiple-piece construction 124
  one-piece construction 124
  pattern drafting 119–20
  preparation 117
  two-piece construction 123
cork leather 105
corn leather 109
cotton 91
CoverBee 145
crossbody bags 29
Cult Gaia 94

D

design education 171
  internships 171–2
design process 41
  design briefs 43
  design considerations 58–65
  design cycle 42
  design development 52–6
  design for disassembly 59, 99

drawing for the design process 69–73
  McCartney, Stella 44–5
  producing a concept 50
  research 46–9
designer bags 15–22
Desserto 108
Diffus Design 135–6, *137*
digital design 84–5
  digital fashion designers 134
  physical or digital portfolio? 178–80
Dior 19, 26, 32, 36, 140
  Dior, Christian 14
  saddle bag 22–3, 32
document holders 35
Dolce & Gabbana 110
drawing 67
  digital toolbox 84–5
  drawing for the design process 69–73
  drawing on the page 74–5
  hand drawing and computer drawing 68
  hand drawing toolbox 83
drawing bags 76
  expanded views 70, 82
  line and shading 78–81
  perspective drawing 76–7
DriTan™ 130

E

earbuds 142, 147
ECCO Leather *64*, 130
edgings 122–3
Ellen MacArthur Foundation 44
embossed leather 102
equipment 118
  computer drawing 84–5
  hand drawing 83
ergonomics 48
ethical production 43
Everpurse 135
eyewear 147, 159–61
  eyewear cases 151

F

Fabricant, The 139
fair trade 96

fanny packs (bum bags) 147, 151
Fendi 19, 20, 25, 28, 36, 60
Ferragamo 109, 116
Fischer, Urs 44
flexible stone 106
footwear 109, 153–7
fourchettes 164
full-grain leather 96

G

genderless bags 36–8
glasses 147, 159
  bridge and bridge box 160
  frames 159
  lenses 159
  temple and temple drop 160
Globe-Trotter 38
gloves 162–4
  anatomy of a glove 164
Google 140
grain (leather) 96, 102
grape leather 113
Gucci 14, 15, 33, 36, 44, 88, 157, 185
  Jackie O bag 15, *17*, 28
gussets 117

H

H&M 36, 44, 107, 113
Hadoro 142
Halston 19
hand-held handbags 26
Hanifa 134
Happy Genie 109
hardware 22, 64–5
Hardy, Françoise 17
headphones 142, 147
heels 154
Hepburn, Audrey 17, 159
Hermès 15, 24, 26, 144, 150, 167
  bag production 128–9
  Birkin bag 19, 32, 36, 129
  Kelly bag 15, 26, 129
hides 101
Hilfiger, Tommy 60–1, 134
Hobo bags 28
hues 63

Hugo Boss 101, 107
Hulanicki, Barbara 17

I

ideas generation 53–4
ideation drawings 69
insole boards 154
iPad cases 145

K

Kaanas 105
Kate Spade 135
Kelly, Grace 15
Kering 44, 183–5
key holders 149
kips 101
Klimek, Alexandra 189–93
KOBA® 45
kombucha leather 110
Kors, Michael 26, 60, 63
Kreafunk 144

L

Lagerfeld, Karl 19, 27
laptop cases 145, 147
lasts 153–4
leather 88, 100
  full-grain leather 96
  tanning 88, 100–1
  types of leather 101–2
  see small leather goods
leather alternatives 103–13
Likarz-Strauss, Maria 11
Lineapelle 64, 96, 185
linings 99
Loewe 18, 29, 32, 34, 91, 142
London College of Fashion 189–90
Longchamp 26, 92
Lorica® 105
Louis Vuitton 17, 20–2, 24, 28, 33, 36, 91, 150, 183
  Horizon Earphones 142
  OLED bags *136*, 137–8
  virtual accessories 139
Lucite 14, 94
Luckynelly 106

luggage 37–9
  luggage tags 147, 149
LVMH 45

M
MAGNETHIK 109
Maison Margiela 36, *95*
Maison Peaux Neuves 113
make-up bags 151
Malai 110, 113
Master & Dynamic 142
materials 63–4, 87, 96
  combining materials 99
  functions of the material 96–8
  leather alternatives 103–13
  linings 99
  main materials for bags 88–95
  reinforcements 98–9
  why leather? 100–2
Matt & Nat 91, 92, 96
McCartney, Stella 44, 50, 92, 96, 107
  brand values 44
  Falabella bag 45, 107
  Frayme Milo bag 45
  sustainable manufacture 44–5
men's bags 31–5
messenger bags 34
microfibre 105
mock-ups 53
monograms 13
mood boards 52
Mulberry 32, 33, *65*, 101, 145, 189
Murakami, Takashi 22
mushroom leather 107, *129*
Mvuemba, Anifa 134

N
nap 102
nappa leather 101
neoprene 95
Newson, Marc 183
Nike 24, 156
Nisolo 88
nubuck 102
NUO 106
nylon 92

O
Oakley® 161
OLED (Organic Light-emitting Diode)
  screens 137–8
one-point perspective 76
orange leather 109

P
Paguro 96, 104
paper leather 110
Parley Ocean Plastic™ 103, 183
passport holders 147, 148
patent leather 102
pattern drafting 119–20
Paul Smith 32, 33, 38
personal branding 185
perspective drawings 76–7
persuasive illustrations 71–2
phone cases 141–2
Piñatex® 107, 108
Poiret, Paul 13
polyester 94
polyurethane (PU) 91–2
portfolios 173
  creating a portfolio 174–7
  physical or digital portfolio? 178–80
  plan in miniature 180–1
  using graphics 180
Prada 19–20, 27, 28, 30, 34, 60, 64, 91,
  92, 101, 145, *149*
  Prada, Miuccia 19
Première Vision 64, 96, 185
presentation sheets 54
Prevolve 157
price range 61
process sketches 70
product development 115, 116–17
  assembly 124
  construction considerations 122–4
  final sample 125
  first sample 120
  pattern drafting 119–20
  preparation 117–18
  sustainable manufacture 126–31
product life cycle 43
professional development 169

design education 171–2
expanding your horizons 183–5
Klimek, Alexandra 189–93
pathway to success 186–8
portfolios 173–82
what makes a successful designer?
  170
prototypes 73
Published By 131
Pucci, Emilio 18
Puma 140
purses 150

Q
Quant, Mary 17, 166
QWSTION 30, 108

R
Rabanne, Paco 17, 167
Ralph Lauren 18, 135
range plans 54–5
raw edges 122
Ray-Ban® 161
recycling 50
regenerative design 58
reinforcements 98–9
rendering 68
research 46
  consumer and market research 49
  primary research 47
  secondary research 47
  technical research 48–9
  trend research 49
  visual research 47–8
reticules 10
Rhino 85
RIMOWA 142
ROKA 161
rubber 104

S
Saint Laurent 26, 155, 185
Samsonite 37, 183
Samsung 138
satchels 30
Schiaparelli, Elsa 13

ScobyTec 110
seams 122–3
seasonality 60–1
Sedgwick, Edie 17
Sex and the City 20, 22
shoes 9, 153–7
    anatomy of a shoe 155
shoulder bags 27
sides 101
signature pieces 116–17
signature prints 19
SKFK 94
skins 101
slow fashion 43
small leather goods 25, 147
    flat accessories 148–9
    three-dimensional accessories 150–1
smart technology 135
    new tech accessories 141–5
    smart accessories 138
    smart bags 135–8
    smart materials 49
smartwatches 144
socks 156
Sole Society 105
soles 155
splitting leather 101–2
Sprouse, Stephen 20
stiffeners 154
Stitch Academy 134
suede 102
sunglasses 147
    anatomy of sunglasses 159
supply chain 43
Supreme *62*
sustainable manufacture 44–5, 126–7
    innovations through technology 130–1
    longevity 128–9
    sustainable design 58–9
synthetic materials 13

T
tablet holders 147
Taikka 107
tanning 88, 100–1
tech packs 56

technical drawings 73
technology and design 133
    augmented and virtual reality 139–40
    digital fashion designers 134
    new tech accessories 141–5
    smart technology in fashion bags and
    accessories 135–8
    sustainable manufacture 130–1
Telfar 38
Thom Browne 36, 38
three-point perspective 76
Tiffany & Co 24, 38, 62, 151
Timberland 88
Tinkercad 85
Tom Ford 35, 145
tones 63
Toray 113
tote bags 26, 33
trade shows 64, 96, 185
tranks 164
tree bark leather 110
turned edges 122
turned seams 123
Twiggy 17
two-point perspective 76
two-tone leather 102

U
Ultrasuede™ BX 113
United Nude 155, 157, *159*
Unseen, The 136–7
upcycling 99
uppers 155

V
van Herpen, Iris 157, *159*
vanishing points 76
VEGEA 113
vegetable tanning 100–1
Vegetan® 105
Veja 109
Victoria Beckham 101
virtual reality 139–40

W
wallets 148

Wang, Alexander 22
weekenders 29, 33
Westwood, Vivienne 96
Whiting & Davis 11–13, 19
women's bags 25–30
wood leather 106

X
XYZBAG 131

Z
zero waste 130
    zero-waste production 50, 130

Picture credits

Drawings by Agnes Virag Moricz unless otherwise specified. 4 Yannis Vlamos/pixelformula/SIPA/Shutterstock; 10 CC0 Paris Musées/Musée Carnavalet – Histoire de Paris; 11 Minneapolis Institute of Art, The Modernism Collection, gift of Norwest Bank Minnesota. Accession Number 98.276.166. Photo: Minneapolis Institute of Art; 12 agefotostock/Alamy Stock Photo; 13 Imperial War Museum © IWM EQU 3967; 14 Clifford Coffin/Condé Nast/Shutterstock; 15 People Picture/TIFF/Shutterstock; 16 Ron Galella/Ron Galella Collection via Getty Images; 17al TopFoto; 17ar Everett Collection Inc/Alamy Stock Photo; 17b Bert Stern/Condé Nast/Shutterstock; 18a Kirstin Sinclair/Getty Images; 18b Photo FIFTH-MAIN/Mark Wahl; 19 Sam Tsang/South China Morning Post via Getty Images; 20 Mary Evans/Everett/Alamy Stock Photo; 21 Pierre Verdy/AFP via Getty Images; 22l Kevin Kane/Wirelmage/Getty Images; 22r Startraks/Shutterstock; 23a Christian Vierig/Getty Images; 23bl Edward Berthelot/Getty Images; 23br Courtesy Chloe. Photo © Nicolas Norblin; 24 Andersphoto/Shutterstock; 26l Courtesy Everlane; 26r Shutterstock; 27l Courtesy JW Pei; 27r Christian Vierig/Getty Images; 28l Agcreativelab/123RF; 28r Photobac/Shutterstock; 29l Vladimir Sukhachev/Shutterstock; 29r Supertrooper/Shutterstock; 30l Courtesy QWSTION; 30r Courtesy The Cambridge Satchel Co; 32 Edward Berthelot/Getty Images; 33l Courtesy WANT Les Essentiels; 33r Courtesy Mulberry; 34l Courtesy Barbour; 34r Msaxalin/Shutterstock; 35l Msaxalin/Shutterstock; 35r DenisNata/Shutterstock; 36 Courtesy xupes.com. Photo: Alice May Photography; 37 CoolPhotoGirl/Shutterstock; 38l Pierre Suu/Getty Images; 38r With permission of Telfar Clemens; 39a & b Courtesy Globe-Trotter; 45 Courtesy Stella McCartney; 47 Kateryna Mostova/Shutterstock; 48 Courtesy VIEW #138 www.view-publications.com. Photographer: Wayta Monzón; 51 Ian Langsdon/EPA/Shutterstock; 52 Eugenia Porechenskaya/Shutterstock; 54-5 © Elleanor Moore; 56 © Annika Andersson; 57 © Serena Bashir; 59 Courtesy JW Pei; 60 gcafotografia/Shutterstock; 61 Jeff Kravitz/FilmMagic; 62 Chesnot/Getty Images; 63 Viktorija Reuta/Alamy Stock Vector ; 64 Courtesy ECCO Leather; 65 Courtesy Mulberry; 69 © Elleanor Moore; 70-2 © Zuxin Qin; 75 © Mendoza Gutierrez; 78 © Maxim Winckers; 83 © Serena Bashir; 85 © Annika Andersson; 89 Courtesy Nisolo; 90 Shutterstock; 91 Courtesy Matt & Nat; 92 Startraks/Shutterstock; 93 Melodie Jeng/Getty Images; 94l Courtesy SKFK; 94r Courtesy Cult Gaia; 95 Courtesy MM6 Maison Margiela; 97 Victor Boyko/Getty Images; 98 Alexeysun/Shutterstock; 99 Mr. Note19/Shutterstock; 102 Courtesy Billy Tannery. Photo: Department Two; 103 Courtesy Parley for the Oceans; 104 Courtesy Paguro; 105 Christie's Images/Bridgeman Images; 106 Courtesy NUO www.nuo-design.com; 107a Courtesy Taikka; 107b Courtesy Stella McCartney; 108a Courtesy Desserto; 108b Courtesy QWSTION; 109 Courtesy Magnethik; 110 Stefania D'Alessandro/Getty Images; 111 Venturelli/Wirelmage/Getty Images; 112 Courtesy Maison Peaux Neuves. Photo: Camille Brasselet; 117 Veronika Synenko/Shutterstock; 118 leungchopan/123RF; 120-21, 125 © Serena Bashir; 127l Courtesy BOTTLETOP; 127r Courtesy Bolt Threads; 128 Sebastien Bozon/AFP via Getty Images; 131 Courtesy XYZ Bag; 135 Bauer-Griffin/GC Images/Getty Images; 136 Thomas Concordia/Getty Images; 137 Courtesy Diffus Design. Design and concept: Hanne-Louise Johannesen and Michel Guglielmi; Project partner: Forster Rohner. Photo: Lisbeth Holten; 138a © 2010-2021 Samsung. All Rights Reserved; 139 Courtesy The Fabricant in collaboration with Zeeuws Museum; 140 Courtesy Wanna; 141 Courtesy Smythson; 142l Mr.Note19/Shutterstock; 142r Ja Crispy/Shutterstock; 143 Bang & Olufsen for RIMOWA, Courtesy of RIMOWA; 144a Hadrian/Shutterstock; 144b kreafunk.com; 145a Courtesy Smythson; 145b Courtesy CoverBee.com; 148a Lemonsoup14/Shutterstock; 148b Early Spring/Shutterstock; 148c Lightman4289/Shutterstock; 149a Courtesy Aspinal of London; 149b MeinaLiao/Shutterstock; 150l Courtesy Aspinal of London; 150r © Maxwell-Scott; 151a AlexandrBognat/Shutterstock; 151b grinvalds/123RF; 151c Jeniffer Fontan/Shutterstock; 152 Victor Boyko/Getty Images;153a Christie's Images/Bridgeman Images; 153b Magdalena photographer/Shutterstock; 154l Retro Ad Archives/Alamy Stock Photo; 154ar Dorling Kindersley/Alamy Stock Photo; 154br xMarshall/123RF; 156a Christian Vierig/Getty Images; 156b xMarshall/Shutterstock; 156c Courtesy United Nude; 157a denisfilm/123RF; 157b Courtesy Code Footwear; 157c Andersphoto/Shutterstock; 158a Courtesy United Nude; 158b Charles Platiau/Reuters/Alamy Stock Photo; 160l kjolak/Shutterstock; 160r visivasnc/123RF; 161 Courtesy ROKA; 162 Pixelformula/SIPA/Shutterstock; 163 Victor Virgile/Gamma-Rapho via Getty Images; 165 Pixelformula/SIPA/Shutterstock; 166l gkm_photoo/Shutterstock; 166r agcreativelab/123RF; 167 Gromovataya/Shutterstock; 172 Courtesy Published By; 174 © Chloe Shinnie; 175 © Elleanor Moore; 176-177t © Maxim Winckers; 177b © Elleanor Moore; 178-9 © Annika Andersson; 180 © Darla-Jane Gilroy; 181t © Sebastian Mendoza Guttierez; 182 © Holly Cowan; 183 Courtesy of Samsonite & Marc Newson Ltd, 2022; 184 Courtesy Troubadour Goods; 185 Shutterstock; 188 Courtesy Maison Peux Neuves. Photo Camille Brasselet.